The Scottish Football Book No 20

Q.P. F.C.
SCOTCH

THE SCOTTISH FOOTBALL BOOK NO 20

Edited by Hugh Taylor

Stanley Paul, London

STANLEY PAUL & CO. LTD.
3 Fitzroy Square, London, W.1
An Imprint of the Hutchinson Publishing Group
London Melbourne Sydney Auckland
Wellington Johannesburg Cape Town
and agencies throughout the world
First published 1974

Printed in Great Britain by offset litho at
Flarepath Printers Ltd., St. Albans, Herts.
and bound by Wm. Brendon & Son,
Tiptree, Essex
ISBN 009 120940 4

CONTENTS

The Editor Says . . . It's all in the Game **7**

The Day the Lions Roared Back **14**

The King of Hearts: Glory Days of Willie Bauld **22**

Sweet and Swing – and Hibernian hit soccer highnotes with an easy beat **29**

Things ain't always what they seem to be – especially in football **38**

Save Our Soccer: Hugh Taylor suggests a face-lift – in style **43**

Big Tam has the last laugh – as Dundee beat Celtic in the League Cup Final **50**

I took one look at you **56**

When the action's red hot **61**

It's that tough quiz for the superior fan **69**

Playground Terrors – and how soccer needs its jesters **75**

Nightmare in the Texaco Cup: Frank Kopel (Dundee United) **80**

Were the old-timers better? **83**

The day I took a bow **88**

The Crusade that failed . . . Celtic victims of European Cup hoodlums **91**

The Players of the Year – they gave us the happiest night of the year **98**

The Happiest Pictures of the Year **101**

The Cup Final Drama **106**

Weep for the Wingers: Jimmy Wilson (Dundee) **112**

Just a Dream Away – Scotland out of luck in the World Cup **118**

The Editor says...
IT'S ALL IN THE GAME

Action . . . humour . . . excitement . . . drama . . . spectacle – our old game of football still contains everything to keep us on our toes at the big match.

So, welcoming you again to yet another Scottish Football Book, I want to let outstanding pictures emphasize that the game isn't dead yet.

Indeed, despite criticism, it's alive and kicking. Didn't Scotland qualify for the World Cup Finals? Didn't Celtic show they are still one of the greatest teams in the world? Aren't we still producing fine players?

Oh, I know many think the Celtic monopoly should be broken. Others feel our efforts at reconstruction, to come into force next season, are too late. And there are the gloomy ones who fear there's not a real challenge at the top in this country.

In this book, you can read about it all – the triumphs, the tragedies, the anxieties.

DETERMINATION – and who's more symbolic of modern football and its competitive spirit than Scotland star Davie Hay, of Celtic, seen here in a tussle with Hibs Jim O'Rourke, another noted player?

Meanwhile, let these pictures say what our great game is still all about. . . .

The feat of the season, of course, was Celtic winning the Scottish First Division title for the ninth successive time. And what more can be said about those fantastic Celts? They are in a class of their own – and Rangers must go on sweating more than ever in their bid to win the championship.

Hibs pipped Rangers for that place in Europe and Tayside had a good season, with Dundee United reaching the cup final and Dundee winning the League Cup.

It was good to see famous old clubs, Airdrie and Kilmarnock, winning their way back to their rightful place in the First Division but sad to realize that Falkirk and East Fife had gone down.

Football, then, is still happy to provide it all – action, thrills, glamour.

I hope this new Scottish Football Book keeps you happy reading about our game of games.

AUTHORITY – and it's Hearts' Ian Sneddon telling his colleagues what to do.

AGILITY – and here you see that splendid young goalkeeper, Ally McLean, of Ayr United, in thrilling action in a match against Clyde.

Far left top: HUMOUR – and it's not nearly as bad as it looks, though Rangers' Derek Johnstone appears here to be putting Bobby Smith's nose out of joint in a tight match with Hibs . . . or you can't really say Jimmy Johnstone, back to his best towards the end of the season, enjoyed having his head imperilled by Gordon Marshall, of Arbroath. No wonder the wee Celtic winger has his hair cut short. . . .

Above: SPEED – and Hibs' Arthur Duncan spanks down the wing with all the grace and pace of an antelope.

Left: RUGGEDNESS – that essential quality in football today is exemplified by the splendid play of Dundee's Ford.

Over: SPECTACLE – and all the excitement is summed up here as Rangers' Cutty Young and Ally Scott make a raid on the Clyde goal – but see keeper Cairney triumphant.

Clydesda

THE DAY THE LIONS ROARED BACK

Suddenly it all came back – all the old Scottish arrogance, artistry and shooting power. And once again Hampden, dripping rain, was a Scottish fortress, grim, grey but triumphant, with the tartan-favoured thousands drunk with emotion and ecstasy, cheering wildly and transforming the bleak day into a festival of colour with flags waving like a field of lilies in the breeze.

The lion had roared back and on 18 May 1974, Scotland beat England 2–0 for one of the sweetest victories. Manager Willie Ormond's team had proved themselves right and proper representatives of Britain in the World Cup.

And those of us who lamented the mediocre form of Scotland only a week before, when the men in blue lost to Ireland at Hampden by 1–0, regretted our lack of faith. Again Scotland proved they were a team for the big occasion. They did well against Czechoslovakia when victory was essential. They played well against West Germany. They played even better against England.

But certainly Willie Ormond, the bright little man who controls our national soccer destiny, must have felt he was entitled to a celebratory gin and tonic after the match.

No-one in football history suffered as much outrageous fortune as the former Hibernian star known affectionately to all as 'the wee man'.

As always, he had been hit by injury. His team had lost to Ireland and he had slammed them for lack of effort, telling them they had played 'the sort of stuff you expect to see on Glasgow Green'. That red-faced occasion was followed by a competent if hardly exciting win over a ramshackle Welsh team, also at Hampden. And, as happens so often to Scotland teams, farce and embarrassment followed.

Down at quiet Largs, their training headquarters, there was a party after the match, followed by a dawn escapade which ended in wee winger Jimmy Johnstone disappearing in a dinghy, with only one oar, as angry Firth of Clyde waves broke over him. Jimmy was rescued but the incident, naturally, made headline news.

Ormond gave 'a wee talk' on discipline and the players really buckled into training. Said Willie, trying to force his usual grin on to that friendly, round face: 'I don't know whether to seek political asylum or settle for an ordinary, old-fashioned asylum'.

The incident, however, worried the fans. Also perturbing was the improved form of England, who had easily beaten Ireland at Wembley on the Wednesday. With Sir Alf Ramsey sacked, extrovert Joe Mercer,

Scotland manager Willie Ormond, the wee man who planned the victory over England.

of Coventry, had become caretaker manager and he was allowing his whiteshirts such freedom of expression that we were reminded again of the halcyon (for England) and frightening (for Scotland) days of Matthews, Finney, Lawton and Co.

Hope was restored when Ormond announced his team. Although the dazzling Tom Hutchison was out because of injury sustained against Wales, the manager had done a fine job. He brought back hotshot Peter Lorimer of Leeds to provide shooting power. And it was a 'champion of champions' team.

Celtic, supreme in Scotland, supplied four players, McGrain, Johnstone, Dalglish and Hay. Leeds, England's best, provided Harvey, Bremner, Lorimer and Jordan.

Mercer had also been crafty. He, too, hadn't been free from fret, for unpredictable Stan Bowles, of Queen's Park Rangers, had taken the huff and stormed out of the England side. Mercer let the Cockney kid go on his merry way and simply brought back 'the ghost', Martin Peters, Spurs veteran whose goal had beaten Scotland at Wembley the previous year.

While all Scotland hoped recent disappointments would be swept away by a fine display, most of the experts thought a draw would be a good result for the home team. And we all hoped to see the emergence of the right pattern to give Scotland a chance in the World Cup in Germany.

The rain couldn't damp the spirits of the 93,271 fans who turned up for the match.

… heroes – red-haired Billy Bremner
…my Johnstone, wearing the jersey
…land goalkeeper Peter Shilton,
…e after the great victory.

The noise was so clamorous that we could almost see it rise in a swirling column into the grey skies. It was, indeed, a fearsome din. Every Scot appeared to be waving a flag and the terracings were a sea of yellow.

Scotland had to make a change just before the game, Martin Buchan, of Manchester United, failing a late fitness test, and John Blackley, of Hibs, taking over, and the teams were:

Scotland: Harvey (Leeds United), Jardine (Rangers), McGrain (Celtic), Bremner (Leeds), Holton (Manchester United), Blackley (Hibs), Lorimer (Leeds), Johnstone (Celtic), Jordan (Leeds), Dalglish (Celtic), Hay (Celtic). Subs: Allan (Dundee), Smith (Newcastle United), Ford (Hearts), Morgan (Manchester United).

England: Shilton (Leicester City), Nish (Derby County), Pejic (Stoke City), Hughes (Liverpool), Hunter (Leeds), Todd (Derby), Channon (Southampton), Bell (Manchester City), Worthington (Leicester), Weller (Leicester), Peters (Spurs). Subs: Clements (Liverpool), McKenzie (Notts Forest), Dobson (Burnley), Watson (Sunderland), Macdonald (Newcastle).

Referee: Van der Kroff (Holland).

The Hampden Roar had returned. That was obvious from the start – and England were upset as they fought nervously to reduce this tribal occasion to the level of a sober game of football.

Impossible!

England's whiteshirted defenders had been in a turmoil from the start and, as the red and yellow banners waved as though the spectators were an army, the marking of the fleeting Scots became haphazard. Scotland surged forward like lions, on top of the world again.

Johnstone and Lorimer may both be right wingers, but with the wee Celt often lying deep, Lorimer combining sweetly with him or drifting left, there was no imbalance. And the tall Jordan had the English in a sweat as he showed he is maturing into a penetrating international leader.

A goal simply had to come. When it did it was tinged with luck but dramatic and deserved for all that. With Bremner splitting the England defence, Shilton had to race out of his goal to frustrate Lorimer. But he could not hold the ball. It rebounded to Jordan and the centre-forward struck it to the empty goal. Would the shot have gone in – or gone past? Arguments are futile. For poor Pejic, playing at Hampden for the first time, lunged at the ball in desperation – and diverted it into the net.

The Scots were so happy they lost their concentration – and that almost cost them a goal when our defence faltered. Weller lobbed the ball forward, Holton missed with his header and Worthington with characteristic confidence volleyed at once. Worthington didn't work wonders this time, to Scotland's relief, for he didn't take enough care and the ball soared over.

Bremner bawled for more action – and the fans got it. Scotland again attacked brilliantly and, with the England defence caught square, Davie Hay enterprisingly snapped up a ball, nipped between Nish and Todd and raced for goal. His great shot would have beaten most keepers – but not the fantastic Peter Shilton, who was to save England from humiliation. The big keeper turned the ball gloriously round the post.

All chants and banners now, the nationalistic crowd gave Scotland tremendous support, Scotland gave the English defence moments of horror – but Scotland nearly gave their foes the equalizer when Harvey lost possession and Holton had to stick out a foot and turn the ball past the post to avert disaster.

Scotland went two up in the 31st minute – again thanks to a deflection. Johnstone brilliantly back-heeled, Lorimer cracked the ball across, Dalglish glided it on – and then the unlucky Colin Todd, trying to clear, deflected the ball past the stranded Shilton.

The Hampden Roar was something to hear now but it turned to a howl when the referee refused to give Scotland a penalty when Hay was tumbled in the box.

This was the best 45 minutes Scotland had played in many years. There may have been a touch of fortune about the goals – but Bremner's boys had been so much on top goals just had to come.

England resumed with Dave Watson in place of Hunter, but it was the super Shilton who saved England in the 51st minute when he made another magnificent save from a splendid Jordan shot.

Johnstone brought the house down with a superb dribble in which he beat three opponents in a couple of yards. And England had another incredible let-off in the 55th minute when a Lorimer free-kick, so fast the ball was blurred, bounced off Shilton – but went past Jordan going in too fast.

England used a second substitute in the 68th minute, pulling off Worthington in favour of Newcastle's Malcolm Macdonald. It made no difference and the game ended as it had begun, with Scotland on the attack

Top right: The goal's on the way. Shilton saves from Peter Lorimer but can only push the ball out to Joe Jordan, whose shot w[illegible] diverted into the net by Pejic.

Right: Jordan watches his shot go in net.

3

ESSO
Bank

and Shilton again saving the day by baulking Dalglish.

So Scotland won 2–0. It could and should have been 4–0. The Hampden hoodoo had been smashed – it was our first home victory over England since 1964 – and England's Joe Mercer gave his rivals full credit. 'The Scots have always impressed me as a fine World Cup team and their performance underlined it against us.' The victory ensured that Scotland shared the home championship with England, but even more important was the manner of the victory, the way Scotland had played.

Ormond had found depth in his pool of players. Blackley was brilliant in place of Buchan, who had done well as deputy for Celtic's George Connelly, out of the reckoning, alas, because of injury. The loss of Hutchison was also overcome. The new front three of Johnstone, Jordan and Lorimer brought back the scoring touch. And Scotland took charge of the middle with the composure which is needed in the World Cup. And the team had learned they had to work.

To me, it was Davie Hay, however, who exemplified Scotland's ability to combine fire with ambition, power and intelligence.

Ormond had found, it seemed, the right formula – the formula which may bring success in Germany – the formula which took the players from that dreadful X-certificate performance when they flopped against Ireland to a seven-day miracle.

As Ormond said: 'It was a good victory but we can do better yet and we should have scored more goals.'

The shooting of Lorimer played a big part. That – and the crowd, the greatest fans in the world. If only we could have taken them all to Germany. . . .

They do as much to worry opponents as Lorimer's shooting, Jordan's buccaneering and Johnstone's endless repertoire of tricks.

Top left: Another English foot gets in the way of a Scottish shot – and Scotland are two up.

Left: Happy faces belong to Jardine, Lorimer, Bremner and Hay – and Scotland have won.

THE KING OF HEARTS – Glory days of Willie Bauld

In these sad soccer days when power is all, formula is the bible, strategy and tactics are computerized and the grey hand of uniformity holds the game in a depressing grip, any scout who recommended a new player on the grounds that he was 'cultured' would be fired on the spot.

Especially if the lad were a centre-forward.

Centre-forwards, you see, are now known as strikers and they are about as artistic as a battering-ram thundering at a fort's brass-bound door. Skill, subtlety, elegance, ball control are four-letter words to managers and modern pundits when strikers are being discussed.

The word 'culture', then, has gone as out-of-date as 30,000 crowds at Rugby Park, Fir Park, Broomfield or any football point more than a mile from Parkhead or Ibrox.

Yet when I look back, there is no doubt in my mind that football falters today because there are too few players who were once symbolic of a game that was almost an art – players to whom flair was all, whose assets were a shrug of the shoulders, the flick of the hip, the dummy, the precision pass, the oily swerve, the beautifully-placed header and the accurate shot, players who were master craftsmen not anonymous, dull destroyers (or ball-winners as they liked to be called).

Players like Willie Bauld, the King of Hearts.

As Hearts celebrate their centenary, thoughts of thousands centre wistfully on Bauld, whose achievements on the field are enshrined in their hearts for ever.

Bauld was perhaps the most cultured centre-forward Scotland has known.

That's not to say he was soft. He wasn't. He could score goals with the best of them, tangle when needed with the toughest defender. But it is for the brilliance of his play, his fascinating footwork, his deft use of the ball, his control, his easy artistry – in vivid contrast to the thumping, charging, rampaging, knock-'em-down tactics of to-day's leaders – that he will be remembered.

Like so many great players, however, Bauld lost out on international honours because he was a contemporary of another magnificent centre-forward, Lawrie Relly, of Hibs.

AN ACE IN THE AIR – that was Willie Bauld, of Hearts. Says Celtic manager Jock Stein: 'Bauld was one of the best headers of the ball I ever saw. He was immaculate in the air. But he never really got sufficient chances at international level to show his worth. Of all the centre-forwards since the war, Willie Bauld was the most natural for the position. His positional sense was uncanny.'

H

And perhaps he might have received even more SFA caps – though to compensate for that Bauld was an automatic choice for Scottish League honours – if he hadn't figured in one of football's most dramatic and unfortunate incidents.

It was Hampden, 1950. *To qualify for the World Cup, Scotland had to beat England and win the home championship. And Bauld had a chance. He went after a fine through-ball. England keeper Bert Williams rashly ran out. And Willie Bauld glimpsed the open goal. Cleverly he flicked the ball over the keeper's head. And Scotland seemed bound for South America and World Cup fame.*

Alas, the ball hit the bar with a crash.

England went on to win 1–0 *and Scotland's World Cup dream was shattered.*

One of those things? Of course it was. Bad luck. But such is East – West rivalry that many blamed Willie for missing the chance. And the Heart was out of favour.

Not that Bauld worried. He was far too good a professional to allow a miss to upset him. And other honours were to come his way – with the only club he really cared for, Hearts.

One of his proudest days was on 23 October 1954. I can never forget his face as he sat in the Hampden dressing-room after the game. Tears poured down his face. His head was aching. His back was bruised. He had pulled a thigh muscle.

He told me: 'This is my happiest day in football.'

A NEW HEARTS IDOL is effervescent Donald Ford, lively, fast, skilful – a Tynecastle leader in the famous old mould.

The tears were tears of joy. His head ached because of the noise of his fans cheering. His back was bruised because of the pummelling he had received as he was congratulated by the Hearts supporters who had invaded the field at the end of the League Cup Final. He had pulled a muscle scoring a glorious goal.

And that 4–2 victory over Motherwell was no ordinary win. It marked a turning point for Bauld and his club and ended the most sorrowful story in football history up till then. Hearts had been the most mercurial team in Scotland. They could play outstanding football. They had produced wonderful teams. But invariably they flopped at the critical time.

Hearts would start well in the League – then fail dismally. They would achieve a notable victory in the Scottish Cup – then go out to some unfashionable club. Not for 48 years had Hearts won a major honour; in 1905–06 they had beaten Third Lanark in the Scottish Final at Ibrox. Since then – failure after failure.

Hearts had become, indeed, the butt of music-hall comedians and the catch-phrase was: 'Is this going to be Hearts' year?'

In 1954, however, Hearts had at last the killer touch. They had great inside-forwards Wardhaugh and Conn. And they had that prince of centre-forwards, Willie Bauld.

Bauld was the hero. In a hurricane start, the blond centre scored twice. His first in nine minutes was a typical Bauld goal.

Winger Souness sent over a fine cross. And you might have thought the ball was attached to a cord leading to Bauld's head. And he was flying, leaping. And his forehead cannoned against the ball. And it was streaking, a speed-blurred blob, into the net.

His second goal was also superb. In a

different mould, though. Just to show Bauld's versatility, ability – and agility. As a flabbergasted Motherwell defence, still dizzy from the first goal, stood still, astonished and indignant at his cheek, Willie juggled like a street corner tanner ba' artist, keeping it up in the air until he placed it exactly as he wanted it.

Then his right foot went back in a flash and he had shot with venomous force and deadly accuracy and once again the ball was streaking like a thunderbolt towards the Motherwell net and again Hastie Weir in goal had no chance as the ball savagely jerked against the netting.

Bauld scored a hat-trick in that game – a game which laid a hoodoo and opened up a new and glorious era in Tynecastle history.

For Willie Bauld, this was the peak of soccer success. For Hearts were the club he dreamed about. He once said:

'Looking back I was certainly a Hearts fan as a kid. Yet in my immature years I think the strong desire to become a well-known player pushed that loyalty into the background. I'm ashamed to admit it but I signed a form for an English club.

'The team was Sunderland. Whether I had committed myself to Hearts or Sunderland first, I can't honestly remember. You

A WIZARD IN ACTION – that's Hearts' dazzling winger, Bobby Prentice, who has played with flair and imagination since joining up at Tynecastle from Celtic.

see, I was signing so many forms and so many scouts were coming to my home.

'I was born in Newcraighall, Edinburgh, and played for the local school. Then I played for Musselburgh Union and I signed for Musselburgh Athletic but never played for them.

'Hearts put me on a provisional form and loaned me out to Newtongrange Star, then to Edinburgh City. What I do know is that I did sign a Sunderland form which said I would have £5 a week. But I also signed for Hearts. How was it sorted out? I don't remember. In fact, it all happened just a few years after the war at a time when signing provisional forms was like signing autographs. Now, of course, the procedure has been tightened up.'

So Willie Bauld, who had been a Bevin Boy, took a full-time job with Hearts. His salary? Just £5 a week.

When Bauld, now a spectator only occasionally at football, looks back, doesn't he wish he hadn't been born so soon? Doesn't he envy the soccer 'millionaires' of today?

He said simply: 'Well, the lads get more today. But I keep thinking how well off I was compared with the players of the generation before mine.'

That was Willie Bauld the player – modest, loyal, a true professional.

He also worked gruellingly hard at football. I wonder how many aspiring youngsters of today would follow his early schedule?

As a Hearts' provisional signing, Willie walked 20 miles every day for more than 18 months. Coaxing him in this stint was George Young, an all-round athlete who had once played Junior football for Dalkeith Thistle.

To vary the routine and perfect his soccer technique, Willie took a ball with him and every mile or so the journey was broken so that George could keep goal as Willie practised shooting and heading.

Ah, those were the days.

In 1962, when Willie Bauld retired after 16 years as a Hearts star, he was asked to choose the best Scotland team from the players of his era.

This was his eleven:

Jimmy Brown (Hearts and Kilmarnock); George Young (Rangers), Willie McNaught (Raith Rovers), John Cumming (Hearts), Willie Woodburn (Rangers), Davie Mackay (Hearts and Spurs); Willie Waddell (Rangers), Jimmy Mason (Third Lanark), Willie Thornton (Rangers), Jimmy Wardhaugh (Hearts) and Davy Wilson (Rangers).

I like it. And I feel this side would do Scotland proud in any World Cup. Yet there's an intriguing point about it. And it shows how times change. For there is not one Celtic player in that splendid combination of power and skill.

Yet Willie Bauld had a great admiration for Celtic. Once he made this significant point – at a time when the Parkhead side weren't in contention for League honours. 'Celtic have always impressed me as being among the best disciplined teams in football and they had personalities, Tully, Haughney, Stein, Evans.'

Bauld must be a prophet as well as a brilliant footballer. Discipline and personality played a great /part in Celtic's triumphs of recent years.

Just, of course, as they played in Hearts' fine run following their 1954 League Cup victory. League flags and Scottish Cup triumph followed and Hearts for a spell were on top of the world.

There were great players, too. But the most famous were the Terrible Trio of

Conn, Bauld and Wardhaugh. How Hearts supporters sigh for stars of that calibre today.

Yet, according to Willie Bauld, although the trio scored around 500 goals among them, they never rehearsed a move before a game. They simply had a natural understanding from the time they were thrown together by that magnificent manager, the quiet, contemplative Dave McLean.

Bauld had this to say of McLean: 'He once told me the most important thing in football was to enjoy playing. How right he was. I enjoyed my football – but I don't think the game is a sport any more. It's too tense and money plays too big a part.'

Let's hope that before long Hearts find a new Willie Bauld, one of the greatest centre-forwards . . . as well as the most cultured.

A NEW STYLE CENTRE-FORWARD is husky Drew Busby, who was signed by Hearts from Airdrie. Drew teams up well with Ford – but he's a striker in the English mould, brave and determined.

SWEET AND SWING – and Hibernian hit soccer highnotes with an easy beat

The skilful, sophisticated football of Hibernian shines brightly in a British soccer world where too many preach the gospel according to muscle.

Not for the Easter Road club power play, unreflective running, high crosses and solid, sweating endeavour. Manager Eddie Turnbull has his players mixing effectively the best of modern play with the grace and spectacle of the past. There are elegance and elan in the heady Easter Road portion – as well as essential drill.

Canny Scots and poetic Irish–Hibernian effectively combine these two national qualities. As their name suggests, Hibs were in origin Irish. Indeed, when they beat Dumbarton to win the Scottish Cup in 1887, on the brake which met the side bringing the trophy in triumph from the west was a notice inscribed on one side: 'Welcome, Hibernian, Winners of the Scottish Cup' and on the other: 'God Save Ireland – Hurray for the Green Jerseys.'

Hibernian still wear green and their romantic ground at Easter Road, wild, windy and grassy, brings a breath of Ireland, while in their quicksilver, interchanging, artistic moves you always sense vivid Irish poetry. But there is also a douce Edinburgh touch, an exemplary orderliness in defence; and the overall effect is a style of play which gains applause from connoisseurs of football in every part of the world.

And how welcome Hibernian football is nowadays when too many teams have no imagination, no stars such as Bobby Johnstone, Jimmy Mason, Torry Gillick, Charlie Tully or George Hamilton who can bring off something different, but rely on fire, stamina and boring lateral play, emphasizing vigour and scorning finesse.

Hibernian refuse to be stereotyped and repudiate the 1970s' insistence on sustained rhythm, high crosses and a win-at-all-costs attitude which forces teams to start from the first minute as though it were the last dying, gasps of the match.

Hibernian do not rely soley on athleticism. They play, indeed, with a tranquillity and switches in style, pace and mood which would gladden the heart of Giacinto Facchetti, captain of Italy and a football intellectual, who says so rightly: 'Good teams change the music, now and again slow it down and suddenly break when the chance occurs.' Hibs do this better than any team in Scotland. But don't imagine for a moment that Hibernian are a 'soft' team. It's true they would have gained even more renown in season 1973–74, especially in UEFA Cup-ties against Leeds United, England's glamour team, whom they were dreadfully unlucky not to defeat convincingly, if they had been sharper near goal and taken more chances so cleverly designed. But Hibernian have always been good fighters.

Manager Eddie Turnbull, inspiration behind Hibernian's success, tells his players exactly what he wants in the extra time of the Drybrough Cup Final. He got it, too. For Hibs beat Celtic.

They had to be. Right from the start there was opposition. In 1875, Hibernian began – as a purely Irish concern. The first captain, Michael Whelahan, was a man proud of his country of origin and it was true Irishmen he liked to have around him. He and the other pioneers of the club were out to establish a team which would command the sympathy and support of the Irish in Edinburgh. They were so Irish to begin with that when they applied for membership in the Edinburgh Association this was refused on the grounds that the club was not 'Scottish in its composition.'

Hibs refused to be daunted. They applied for membership to the Scottish Football Association, were admitted – but not allowed to take part in the Scottish Cup, as only purely Scottish clubs were then considered eligible to compete in a national competition.

Hibs fought on and eventually won the day – then had the satisfaction of beating Dumbarton to take the Scottish Cup in season 1886–87 at Hampden Park.

For years, however, there was an Irish flavour about the club and their best players were of immigrant stock – the giant Tobin in goal, the sturdy backs Lundy and Fagan,

Far right: A stout Hib – sweeper John Blackley.

Right: A prince of scorers – that's Alan Gordon, of Easter Road fame.

Keep an eye on tall Tony Higgins. He's a Hibernian youngster going places.

the powerful half-backs McGhee and McGinn. In the early days Easter Road was known as Hibernian Park. And most of the supporters cheered on their favourites with a brogue in their voices.

Now, of course, Hibernian are as Scottish as porridge or bagpipes and practically everyone of their famous players – and how many stars Easter Road has thrilled to! – owes his birth and allegiance to this country.

The Irish influence, however, must not be forgotten, for that original strain undoubtedly can still be seen in the football sweet as the music of the harp of Tara which so often earns enthusiastic applause when Hibs are at their best.

The stern competitive spirit Hibernian always bring to their football can also be traced to their background. Not entirely to their Irish temper. But to enthralling, no-punches-pulled encounters through the years with their great rivals, Hearts.

Hibs came up the hard way, especially when they played their Tynecastle foes.

You had to be tough in those days. For instance, the two clubs met in the final of the Edinburgh FA Cup in 1878. It was so intensely fought that it required five meetings before it was decided – and the series ended with members of the Hearts side running for their lives from the Hibs

Top right: Hibs and Celtic have had many stern battles recently. Here's an exciting moment from the Drybrough Cup Final as keeper Jim McArthur sees the ball go past, with Celtic's Ken Dalglish looking on.

Right: Hibs centre-half Jim Black clears neatly in a match against Celtic.

Ian Munro, a talented versatile Hibernian player, signed from St Mirren.

supporters and a hansom cab being wrecked in the chase.

Artistic football, however, has for years been Hibernian's trademark. Their Famous Five forward line of Smith, Johnstone, Reilly, Turnbull and Ormond fertilised our soccer with original ideas and even then swung the emphasis away from speed, force and stamina on to skill.

And nowadays Willie Ormond is making attack the keynote in his plans for the Scotland team while Eddie Turnbull guides Hibs to the top with the accent on fine, flowing, attractive football.

'You must always take advantage of the break,' insists the Easter Road manager. 'Even when you are forced to defend you must be looking for a way to attack.'

And how true Eddie's words are! It was an incredible break that won for Hibs the Drybrough Cup at Hampden on 4 August 1973.

A great game had stretched to the last minute of extra time. The crowd of 42,204 who had seen brilliant football were speculating about the 10 players who might be faced with the task of taking penalty kick deciders.

But Celtic were attacking fiercely and Hibs sighed with relief as shots from Dalglish and Hood were blocked.

Suddenly – Hibs broke. Tall Tony Higgins saw his chance and raced upfield. His colleagues had read the move well. The fascinating Alex Cropley had darted into position. Higgins passed, Cropley ran on, then turned the ball smoothly into the path of Alan Gordon.

The fair-haired striker wasted no time and hammered a splendid left-foot shot past the helpless Alistair Hunter in the Celtic goal.

With only 40 seconds left for play in extra time, Hibernian had won with a wonderful goal, perfectly designed and lethally executed. A goal Hibs have scored so often. A goal typical of their style, of their astonishing change in pace.

It was the Drybrough Cup for Hibs for the second year in succession – and the previous season they had also beaten Celtic in extra time.

For manager Eddie Turnbull, it was his third trophy in a row. Only three years in existence, the Drybrough Cup was first won by Aberdeen, with a team moulded by Turnbull, who had just left for Easter Road. Then Turnbull's Hibs won it twice in a row.

In contrast, the Drybrough Cup carried disappointment for Celtic and manager Jock Stein. The Scottish champions had been beaten in all three finals.

The teams in what had proved to be one of the finest games of the season were:

Hibs: McArthur, Bremner, Schaedler, Stanton, Black, Blackley, Edwards, Higgins, Gordon, Munro, Duncan. *Subs.:* Cropley, Smith.

Celtic: Hunter, McGrain, Hay, Murray, McNeill, Connelly, McLaughlin, Dalglish, Lennox, Callaghan, Lynch. *Subs.:* Hood, Brogan.

Although Hibs lost their grip on the League Cup, being beaten by Rangers, and were defeated in the UEFA Cup by Leeds, who won on penalties, the future is brighter than ever – because Hibs have style, class – and faith in themselves and manager Eddie Turnbull.

They play, you see, with an easy beat, a fine mixture of sweet and swing which has them hitting football's high notes.

Left: Hot action as Celtic battle with Hibernian. This time John Blackley is first to the ball as Celtic's Bobby Lennox dashes in and goalkeeper Jim McArthur watches anxiously.

Happy grin from Hibernian manager Eddie Turnbull as he holds aloft the Drybrough Cup.

THINGS AIN'T ALWAYS WHAT THEY SEEM TO BE... Especially in football

Or – who said the camera never lies?

Now and again we look at a picture – and wonder just how true it is.

From last season's hectic action in Scottish football, we select a few photographs to make you smile.

And let's be honest, what you think you see really didn't happen. It merely looks worse because of the angle from which the photographer took his snapshot.

Left: Of some action at a match, you often say: It was hair-raising. But Celtic's Kenny Dalglish's hair isn't rising in fright here because of what he thinks manager Jock Stein will say to him about missing this cross in a match against Hibs. It's the high wind, lashing rain and spectacular jump which has caused Kenny's locks to resemble something out of a Hammer film.

Right: Did you ever say to your chum at a match: 'That one needs a good kick up the backside to waken him up?' Well, one star goalkeeper who is seldom criticised by the fans is Alan Rough. But here the Partick Thistle star seems to be receiving rough treatment. Wee Tom McLean, of Rangers, isn't, however, administering a good kick on the bottom to Alan. He has just missed connecting with the ball, safely gathered by Rough.

5

Left: No, Partick Thistle's Andy Anderson isn't a ju-jitsu expert – and, no, he hasn't cleverly sent Rangers' Alex O'Hara flying with a cute hand jab. Alex has merely made a daring but futile jump to try to head a goal.

Bottom left: Rangers' Ally Scott has played Rugby – but he isn't really trying to hand off Jim Cant, of Hearts, in this match. It's just another of those amazing camera shots which aren't what they seem to be . . . we hope!

Below: 'Hey, mind my nut,' says Derek Parlane of Rangers as Billy McNeill, of Celtic, makes a clearance in an Old Firm game, but there was no danger, really, to Derek's head.

What's going on here? Is referee Alistair McKenzie performing a conjuring trick during an Old Firm game? No, indeed. It's his way to calming a heated scene – before booking Celtic's Davie Hay.

SAVE OUR SOCCER: Hugh Taylor suggests a face-lift – in style

'To be a success in football,' said Joe Mercer, the English manager who has kept at the top despite heartbreaks, 'you must be an eternal optimist.'

It was difficult, however, in season 1973–74, to be optimistic about the state of the game in Scotland. Despite our team's success in the World Cup qualifying series, there was depression everywhere. Gates were still falling. Moans continued about too much negative football. Talk of reconstruction filled the air. The SFA gave permission for senior soccer to be played on the Sabbath, a concession which brought the John Knox out in many kirk-goers.

But for too many once fervent fans football had lost its appeal. And most laughed at the long debates on reconstruction, on super leagues and streamlined competitions. They had heard it all before – for countless years, indeed, years filled with talk but no action, years in which our football slithered deeper into trouble.

Twenty years ago, in the first Scottish Football Book, I wrote that 'probably most of the smaller clubs would fare better financially if they reverted to Junior status. But many would rather close down than step down. And who can blame them? It is not their fault that they have not the population to allow their teams really to flourish. Yet these small clubs are becoming outdated. How, then, can they be kept alive? Smaller Leagues – that's the answer. Many legislators consider the present Leagues – A and B Divisions – are too unwieldy. If three divisions were formed and more cup competitions arranged there would be greater interest maintained right through the season.'

And a year later, in the Scottish Football Book of 1956–57, I wrote:

'In this modern age we are watching more football than ever now that floodlighting is becoming commonplace. We must beware, however, that we do not have too large an appetite. Clubs must realise that big names, exotic names from Brazil and Hungary, Russia and Peru, are not enough to attract huge attendances. They must continue to strive to improve the standard of play. The fan is becoming more particular. He wants to see good football, no matter who is playing.'

As I say, that was written 20 years ago.

It still holds good today.

Have we progressed ? No indeed. Why, floodlights were banned because of a power crisis. There was far too much football – and, in one spell, Celtic had eight important games in 17 days. Clubs still squabbled about the size of proposed new leagues, though the new super league due in season 1975–76 may take a trick.

And the crowds became even smaller. Clubs which attracted 10,000 to 12,000 fans

SACRIFICES must be made to make football more attractive – that's the view of Celtic manager Jock Stein.

20 years ago were happy if 5,000 turned up for a game.

There was no more talk, however, about second division clubs becoming junior. Times had changed and so had social conditions. There was more money about. Most clubs now had diversions, paying diversions, social premises, for instance, and they were paying their way to their own satisfaction if not striking serious blows for Scotland's football prestige.

Was there a cure for football's ills? The men at the top had their own ideas. Here were the views of:

Jock Stein, Celtic manager: The only way to nurse the game back to prime condition is to make the professional clubs viable by ensuring big crowds. The game is what counts and so sacrifices must be made. The system must be changed – for more than half the teams in Scotland don't have a chance of challenging for the honours.

Jock Wallace, Rangers manager: We must go for more attacking football. That's the only way to get the crowds back to the game. Today far too much emphasis is placed on defence. The tensions are still the same. Players are still desperate to win. But bigger crowds are needed to stimulate them, make them more aggressive and add to their will to win. Play fast, open attacking football and the crowds will come back.

Hugh Nelson, SFA president in season 1973–74: We need success in the World Cup to restore pride in Scottish football. Interest would be aroused again and gates would go up. At home, co-operation must be the keynote. All clubs must get together to try to improve the system and we must also try to make football more attractive – by playing attacking football.

Willie Ormond, Scotland team manager: I would love to see a mass departure from defensive football. We need natural players but I am concerned when I see schoolboys playing 4-2-4 or 4-3-3. Boys of that age should be encouraged only to express themselves naturally. I want to see less coaching where our kids are concerned. Let them develop natural ball skills first.

Nothing new there, of course. But who was going to do anything about it? Action – that's what Scottish football needed.

Was football too commercial? That has always been a moan by some people in Scotland and a school of thought has it that the game will never be right until all the clubs are, like Queen's Park, amateur. On the other hand, influential administrators believe there can't be too much sponsorship and League secretary Tommy Maule advocates:

'More sponsorship. Tournaments like the Texaco Cup are among the highlights of the season. Sponsorship not only supplies financial benefit to a competition, it also injects a bright and breezy atmosphere which heightens everyone's interest. I'd like to see our League Cup become the next competition offered to prospective sponsors.'

While others, still Corinthian at heart, feel sponsorship is an evil and that football should be big enough to support itself, there is no doubt that big business can help modern sport.

Take the Prudential Assurance Company, for instance. A relative newcomer to sports sponsorship, it has decided to spend around £30,000 on tennis competitions. In 1972, business and commerce spent around £7 million on direct sponsorship of sport, and associated indirect costs brought total expenditure on this relatively new medium to about £17 million. And the figure is steadily rising.

But football doesn't do all that well and, in these modern times when recognition of cash problems usually overwhelm all scruples, there seems to me to be no reason why more and more giant firms shouldn't give soccer a helping hand – and gain themselves considerable publicity.

Even Mr Mercer's eternal optimist, though, would concede that these ideas and plans have not solved the problem of Saving our Soccer.

Perhaps it's too late. Perhaps the great love of football, so devotedly shown in the 20s, 30s, 40s and 50s, has turned to ashes. Perhaps the new way of life has finished for all time the resolve of thousands to see their team at all costs. More people play games themselves on Saturdays. More wives, fiery with women's lib, demand that husbands accompany them on shopping expeditions, help in the house or take them for a run in the car. And the lazier folk just turn on television.

I am a romanticist. I still believe – although I have no proof – that the real cure for our football illness is to play as we used to play – with verve, love, flair, beauty, art, with cavalier outlook. Fans would come back if we wiped the fear out of football, the fear which means packed defences, violence, cynicism and an outlook which

O ESSO

Left: STYLE must be brought back – style as shown by Alfie Conn of Rangers and Alec Cropley of Hibs.

says that not losing is everything, instead of attempting to win by playing skilful/football.

In England they are at last realizing that attacking football does not only pay, it attracts fans. While physical commitment has always been part and parcel of the British game, skill is still what matters most and an improvement in manners and morals will help the gates. Let's get rid, too, of that terrible word, 'professionalism', which seems to me to be a nauseating euphemism for cynical, dirty play.

After all, football is more than a sport to most of us in Scotland, especially those of us who were brought up in the old days when Saturday afternoon was the highlight of a dreary week, when our only heroes were the men in the colourful jerseys, when football was theatre, church, cinema, parliament all in one.

Our main trouble is that we have stopped recognizing the beauty in football – the athletic perfection of a McGrory hurtling through the air in a daredevil attempt to reach a cross, the aesthetic satisfaction of watching a James, Mason, Gillick, Venters, White controlling a football, the entrancing sight of Ajax, Real Madrid, the Hungarians, the old Hibs and Spurs sides, in full attack.

ATTACK and attack and attack – with more accent on aggression, football will improve, says Rangers' manager Jock Wallace, seen here proving his point as he welcomes Doug Houston, once of Dundee, to Ibrox . . . for Doug relishes an attacking game.

Too many modern experts do not recognize beauty as being important. They prefer a robot-like approach, a mathematical outlook. They may say 'Oh, very nice' of a move by Best (alas, no longer with us) or Ken Dalglish or the Brazilians but they don't feel their job is to encourage that sort of thing. It would be too dangerous, might fail. Solid citizens – that's what they're after. They'd rather pack a defence than take a chance with a solo at which Patsy Gallagher was so adept.

Laugh at me if you like. But I still maintain that a return to football with style and vivacity, with eagerness and gallantry, will do more to save the game than a thousand meetings, a thousand suggestions for reconstruction.

History proves my point.

Away back in 1698 M. Misson, a Parisian visitor to England, was writing: 'En Hiver le football est un exercise utile et charmant' – In Winter, football is a useful and charming exercise. Note the word 'charming' – even then football had beauty.

And in 1581 Richard Mulcaster stressed the importance of style in the game, writing: 'The football, play which could not possibly be growne to this greatness that it is now at nor have bene so much used, as it is in all places, if it had not had great helpes both to health and strength. Yet it must be civil and rash running and too much force oftentimes breaketh some inward conduit and bringeth ruptures.'

Let us stop stamping out individualism. We do not need new patterns of play. Increased emphasis on skills, on style, on character – that's the way to better football and bigger gates.

When we no longer sneer that a player like Cruyff who dribbles and splits defences is anachronistic, we will be on the way back.

ARTISTRY will aid soccer – and who is more artistic than George Connelly of Celtic?

BIG TAM HAS THE LAST LAUGH – as Dundee beat Celtic in the League Cup Final

The widest grin in Scotland lit up the chilly, depressing afternoon of Saturday, 15 December 1973. It belonged to Tommy Gemmell, buccaneering captain of Dundee. Never had swashbuckling Gemmell been happier. A dream had come true. He had led Dundee to victory in the Scottish League Cup Final.

And the club they had just beaten were none other than the team with whom Gemmell had found fame but who had allowed him to leave – Celtic.

'I was so overjoyed at this win,' said big Tam, 'that I jumped into the bath at the end with my strip still on.'

Gemmell had every reason to celebrate. He had also been one of the few people in Scotland to forecast a Dundee victory.

A few days before the final he said: 'Everyone knows how I feel about this game. It would be a fairy tale, Snow White and the Seven Dwarfs stuff, if Dundee win. Well, no-one played harder for Celtic than I did but I would love to put one over them in the final.'

Then Tom went on to explain the reasons – backed by every neutral football enthusiast in the country – why it would be good for the game if Dundee took the trophy.

'Celtic,' he said, 'are always winning things. We at Dundee would get more out of a win than Celtic. Dundee has gone to sleep this season over football. If we win, we might wake up the fans and bring them back to the game.'

There's no more outrageous extrovert in football than Gemmell and he added, straight-faced: 'The pressure is on Celtic. They have lost the last three League Cup finals and this is a jinx match for them.'

But the flamboyant big fellow with the laughing eyes and hawk nose found few supporters even in Dundee. Celtic, as always, started hot favourites. Surely, said their supporters, we can't lose four finals in a row?

Celtic, indeed, had an astonishing record. This would be their tenth successive League Cup Final. They lost the first of these, won the next five, then were defeated in the last three. But they had played in devastating fashion to destroy arch-rivals Rangers in the semi-final, while Dundee had struggled against Second Division Kilmarnock in their semi and won luckily by 1–0 – thanks to a fine shot from the man himself, Tommy Gemmell, scoring his first goal for Dundee –

Top right: As flamboyant, as spectacular as ever, Dundee captain Tommy Gemmell clears with all his old dashing style in the League Cup Final against his old club, Celtic.

Right: Dundee celebrate their League Cup victory with champagne in the bath at Hampden – and Tom Gemmell is so happy he plunges in without stopping to remove his strip.

VISIONHIRE

and then making two valiant goal-line clearances as Kilmarnock stormed in at the end.

The betting was one to two on Celtic, six to four against Dundee, which showed how those experts, the bookmakers, felt about it.

Dundee, it was true, had reached the final without losing a tie but, as even Gemmell admitted, they had been blessed with good luck – and the scoring touch of Gordon Wallace, who had notched six of the 20 goals. Celtic had scored 23 goals in 12 ties – they lost once to Rangers and once to Motherwell – and Bobby Lennox was top scorer with six.

So few people in the miserably small crowd of 27,974 at Hampden that dreary December day gave Dundee much chance.

It was, indeed, a sad climax to what should have been one of our most glamorous competitions.

Although legislators had tried to brighten it by playing under the experimental laws of no offside between extended 18 yardlines, the tournament had dragged on and on.

And because of a national fuel emergency the Government had banned floodlighting.

It was, then, an early reveille for the fans, for the game had to kick off at 1.30 pm to allow for an extra 30 minutes if needed. The Government had announced a ban on generators and that meant an end to any attempts to play under floodlights. There were suggestions that the final be postponed until later in the season so that the game could be played in daylight but, in the end, it was decided that the final must be played on 15 December.

There was more trouble when the teams arrived early at Hampden. Both protested that the game should not be played because of the dreadful Arctic conditions. Managers Jock Stein, of Celtic, and Davie White, of Dundee, thought the pitch wasn't playable and considered the fans shouldn't have to stand on snowbound terracings.

Despite the snow, referee Bobby Davidson declared the pitch playable – and so the game went on before the lowest attendance at Hampden for a major final since the war.

Everyone, however, had the shivers as the teams lined up like this:

Celtic: Hunter, McGrain, Brogan, McCluskey, McNeill, Murray, Hood, Hay, Wilson, Callaghan, Dalglish. *Subs.:* Johnstone, Connelly.

Dundee: Allan, Wilson, Gemmell, Ford, Stewart, Phillip, Duncan, Robinson, Wallace, Scott, Lambie. *Subs:* Johnstone, I. Scott.

Referee: R. H. Davidson, Airdrie.

The match was played in continuous sleet and rain. The pitch was bone hard underneath yet coated with a top of shallow mud. The same for both sides, of course – but Dundee adapted much better to the conditions. On the sodden field, the men from Dens Park kept the blue bonnets of their fans in the air with nippy football.

The neat touches of Duncan (a player on whom Celtic had cast envious eyes), Wallace, Scott and Lambie continually had the Celtic defence off balance and their stout defenders were never as troubled as were their Celtic counterparts.

Top left: One of the dangerous Celtic raids in the League Cup Final – but Dundee keeper Thomson Allan is on the spot to save.

Left: The goal that won the League Cup, beautifully scored by Dundee's Gordon Wallace.

In complete contrast to the clever one-touch play of Dundee, Celtic by-passed the middle with long passes, trying to spring Wilson, Dalglish and Hood and seeking to take advantage of the offside experiment. But Dundee covered too closely for Celtic to get away with that little scheme.

Although it was never a classic, it was an intriguing game, skilfully enough played despite the atrocious weather and pitch.

The writing was on the ball early for Celtic, whose fans were muttering sadly about hoodoos with the final hardly begun. As the fifth minute approached, Jocky Scott broke speedily on the right and found Gordon Wallace inside. The ball went to Duncan and Dundee were in with a great chance of opening the scoring – until Duncan shot too high. Then, in the 15th minute, as Wallace chased a Duncan pass, goalkeeper Ally Hunter advanced and missed the ball. Fortunately for Celtic, Danny McGrain was on the line to clear. The trend was clear – that Dundee had no inferiority complex and that Celtic weren't playing well – as Scott and next Lambie shot and gave Hunter no end of worry before the dangers were averted.

Confusion reigned in the Celtic defence. Once the ball struck Jim Brogan's arm and there were Dundee appeals for a penalty, brushed aside firmly by the referee.

It was 30 minutes before Celtic settled and began to find their form.

Half-time arrived with Celtic in better mood but with Dundee unlucky not to be ahead.

They must have been apprehensive about the second half, annoyed because they hadn't grabbed their chances. And only two minutes had gone when Harry Hood beat two defenders and set up a fine chance for Dalglish. But the shot went straight to the arms of goalkeeper Thomson Allan.

Water began to appear on the pitch and play became a gamble, with the ball unpredictable, sometimes shooting violently off the slippery turf, at others becoming trapped in the mud.

And then Dundee won the final with a spectacular goal Pele would have envied.

It was a goal that surely must have ended Dundee's reputation as being a mystery team. For years they had been noted for entertainment, artistic play and entertaining touches. But they had all too often lacked the killer touch.

It was a goal that showed Gordon Wallace to be among the best forwards in Britain.

The game was into its 76th minute and it seemed to be deadlocked. Then Paul Wilson conceded a free kick near the centre-circle. Bobby Wilson took the kick. The ball was dropping near Celtic's penalty spot. Beating all the defenders, Wallace, facing his own goal, superbly breasted the ball down, turned and swept the ball magnificently into the net past the helpless Hunter.

It was the type of goal Pele, that Brazilian immortal, loved to score and it brought desperately needed glamour as well as victory for Dundee to the League Cup Final.

That was the end. Celtic hit back hard, as always. They brought on substitutes Jimmy Johnstone and George Connelly for Hood and Hay respectively. A Murray header went near. Johnstone came down in the penalty area – but he had tumbled over the legs of Dalglish.

Dundee held out – and deservedly took the League Cup back to the jute city.

The Wallace goal made the final. And Dundee deserved their victory for they were the better, sharper and more flexible team, deadly on the break, making fine use of the ball.

But the game on a dismal day should be a lesson to football's leaders. It was a pathetic affair. Cup final days should be days of blazing excitement, with the sun shining and the flags proudly fluttering and the fans in their tens of thousands making the atmosphere electric.

Certainly they should never be played in December – but it's up to the legislators to ensure that our fiesta days are in spring or autumn.

For Tommy Gemmell, though, that dull December day would always be as fragrant as a June afternoon.

He picked up not one but three winners' medals after the match. 'In addition to lifting my fifth League Cup badge, I received two League Championship medals,' he said. 'They were passed on to me as I hadn't collected them in my last couple of years at Parkhead.'

And then that big grin broke out again.

'I've had many great days in the game,' said Tom, 'but it was wonderful to take the League Cup – and wave it at the Celtic fans.'

Few would grudge Gemmell, one of the game's few remaining characters, his moment of glory. . . .

Or the last laugh over his old chums of the club who thought he had no more to offer them.

I TOOK ONE LOOK AT YOU

That's the title of an old, old song. It could also be a signature tune in football. For how often have you seen a look that speaks so much louder than words or action?

Football is a game of high tension, of emotion. A game in which it is impossible to hide your feelings. A game in which, during the heat of the moment, passion comes to the surface.

Players are like actors. Nowadays the game is becoming show-business and players play all kinds of parts.

Perhaps they talk too much. Perhaps they glare too much. Perhaps they show too much exuberance when a goal is scored, too much despair when a goal is lost.

But it's all part of the game – and, come on, now, don't we really enjoy all these facets of human emotion so vividly portrayed in a glance on the soccer field?

Just what a look can say is revealed in these pictures. . . .

Right: THE LOOK that says: Oh, God, why did you make me a goalkeeper? And all the dejection in the world is on the face of Partick Thistle goalkeeper Alan Rough just after Rangers have scored a late goal.

THE LOOK that says: Don't be daft. And Celtic's Jim Brogan makes sure by his expression that goalkeeper Alistair Hunter will, indeed, 'Let the ball go past'.

Left: THE LOOK that says: Oh, what a referee. And angry Hearts' players Alan Anderson and Jim Brown portray the feelings of men who are convinced they have been the victims of dreadful injustice – this time by the award of a penalty against them in a match with Rangers.

Bottom left: THE LOOK that says: I've made my mind up. And referee Alistair McKenzie refused to listen to appeals by Celtic colleagues not to take the name of Davie Hay after an incident in an Old Firm game.

Below: THE LOOK that says: How the heck did you let that one in. And Rangers' defender Tom Forsyth doesn't have to say anything to express his feelings after Celtic have scored. That look says it all.

THE LOOK that says: We've scored. And THE LOOK that says: Well, it wasn't my fault. Rangers' Alfie Conn shows jubilation as Celtic keeper Alistair Hunter and full-back Danny McGrain try to explain things to colleagues who want to know why a mistake was made.

WHEN THE ACTION'S RED HOT

Football can be all things to all men. Some of us like our soccer sweet and stylish and prefer the subtleties of an Alex James, the oily swerves of a Tommy Walker, the polish of a Jimmy Mason and the wizardry of a John White and the leisurely, artful devices of the master inside-forward of yesterday.

Others insist that football is a game of tough physical challenge and they relish the fierce onslaughts of a Jimmy Smith, a Jimmy McGrory, a Derek Parlane or Billy Houliston, the clanging tackles of a Dave Mackay, the powerful clearances of a George Young or Davie Lapsley.

No matter our preferences, one thing is certain. Football still thrills most spectators because of action, red-hot action, action

HEY, MIND MY HEAD, snaps Rangers' Billy Mathieson as all the stops are pulled out by Jimmy Johnstone of Celtic and his attacking mates as they try to storm the Ibrox defence in yet another nerve-tingling Old Firm clash.

that has you on your toes, cheering, your heart pounding.

And despite complaints that new tactics and defensive complexes makes enjoyment less for the fans, we in Scotland continue to applaud attacking, flowing football, football laced with skill. . . .

And, of course, RED HOT ACTION which keeps football as the world's premier sport.

Our photographers who are always nearest the action, who brave cold, rain, sleet, snow, wind and mis-directed shots, once again bring you dramatic pictures from the Scottish scene in this soccer spectacular.

A MID-AIR twist by Clyde goalkeeper Phil Cairney brings an Ayr United raid to an end and the acrobatic goalie gets a big cheer.

Right: JACK IN THE BOX? No, it's high-jumping Davie Robb, of Aberdeen, really getting up for a header in a match against East Fife.

RICULTURAL
OTOR ENGINEE
KIERIE GARAGE.

Left: I'LL GIVE YOU A HAND, BOBBY – that's what Celtic's Dixie Deans appears to be saying as he goes up with Aberdeen keeper Bobby Clark in an exciting game at Pittodrie.

Bottom left: GRIMLY DETERMINED is Ayr United goalkeeper Alistair McLean who saves the day for his side in face of an all-out Clyde onslaught.

Below: A STERN BATTLE OF WILLS in this picture – and it's won by Dundee goalkeeper Thomson Allan, who clears from Celtic's Dixie Deans.

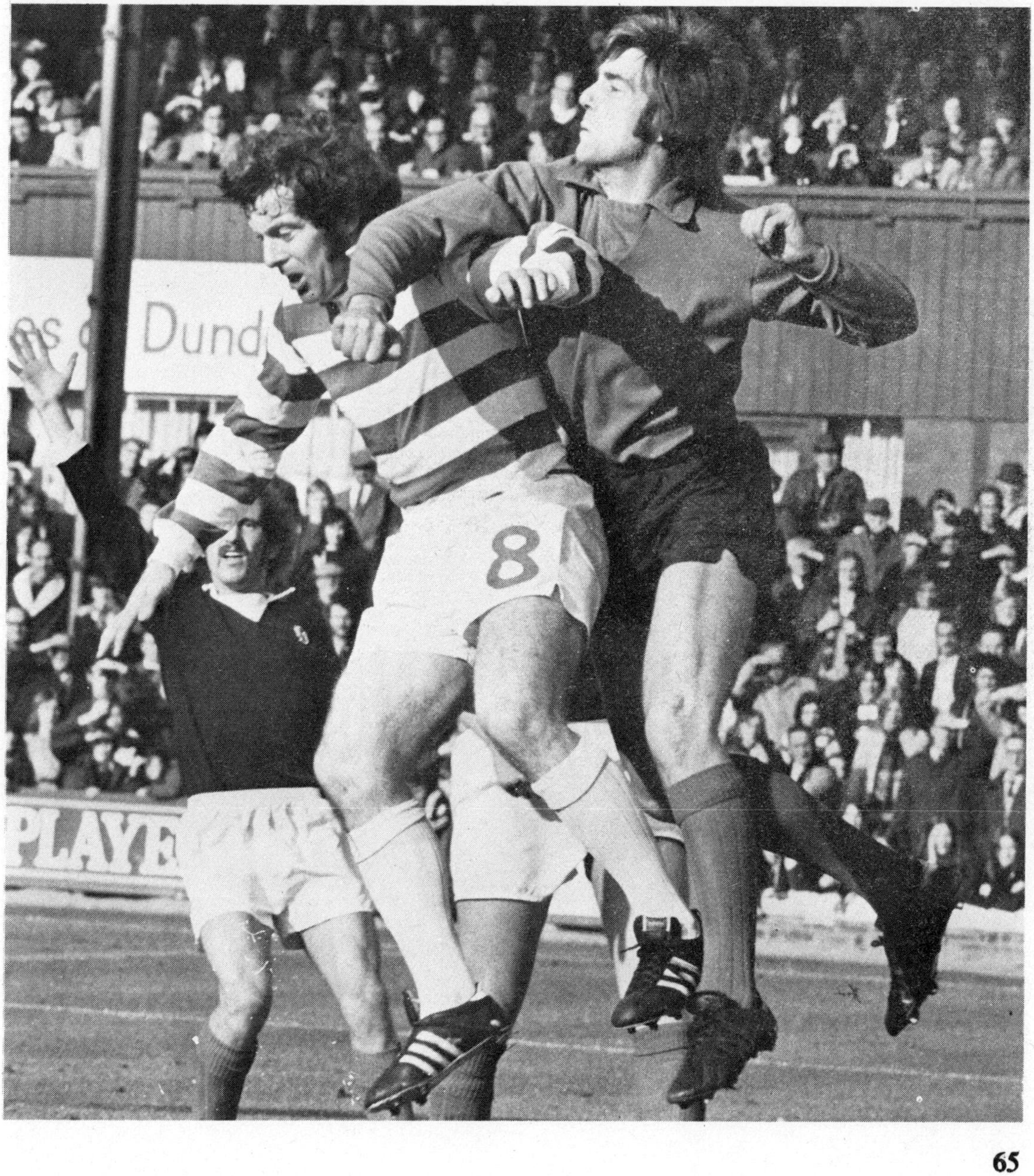

OUT OF MY WAY, SON – and Aberdeen's Willie Miller storms past Quinton Young, of Rangers, with hands apparently playing a a vital role in this duel.

Left: NO ONE DRAWS BACK in an Old Firm encounter and here you see Billy McNeill, Celtic captain, and Alex MacDonald, of Rangers, in a dour joust for the ball.

WINTER WONDERLAND? Hardly. But soccer in the snow goes on and Harry Hood of Celtic gets in a shot against Dundee United on a slippery pitch.

IT'S THAT TOUGH QUIZ FOR THE SUPERIOR FAN

REFEREE QUIZ

Here it is again – the tough quiz for superior football fans only. So you're good. So you think the referee's a mug.

Well, just what would you do if you were the referee. . . .

1. When a goalkeeper suddenly loses his temper with an opponent who has been needling him during the game and throws the ball violently at him while the opponent is standing outside the penalty area?

Is the correct decision a penalty kick – or a direct free kick outside the penalty area?

2. When a player taking a penalty kicks the ground and moves the ball only a few yards – but follows up and scores with a second kick?

Do you order the kick to be re-taken – or award a free-kick to the defenders?

3. When a defender, taking a direct free-kick outside the penalty area, passes the ball back to his goalkeeper – and is annoyed to see the keeper miss the ball and lets it go into the net?

Would you award a goal, order the kick to be re-taken – or give a corner-kick ?

4. When a player tries to land a left-hook on an opponent – but fails to make contact?

Should you send the offender off – or take no action?

5. When a goalkeeper accidentally strikes an opponent when trying to punch the ball clear?

Do you take no action – or award a penalty kick.

6. When a loudspeaker relays the half-time scores with the second half in progress?

Is the correct decision to take no action – or stop the game and tell the home officials the noise must be stopped?

Now here are a couple of really tricky posers.

7. A penalty kick has been awarded. As the kick was taken, one of the attacking team took up position outside the penalty area but in line with the six-yard line. The kick was converted.

Later in the game it happened again. This time, though, the ball rebounded from the bar, the player at the edge of the area gained possession and scored.

Is he off-side?

8. The centre-forward has the ball. He dashes on and he has only the goalkeeper to beat. It looks a certain goal but a defender fouls him and down crashes the centre. But he jumps back to his feet, regains the ball, darts on and scores. But the referee up with play has whistled for a foul.

What's the decision? A penalty kick or a goal?

9. Let's end this part with a quick one. A shot going well past hits the referee and goes into the net.

Is it a goal?

LET THE PICTURES TEST YOUR SOCCER KNOWLEDGE

Football heroes come and go. But long after someone leaves a club to join another or retire his praises are still sung. So we start our picture quiz with a do-you-remember department.

1. Once he was a big favourite with the Easter Road fans. Now he plays in England. What's his name and what's his club?

2. Not so long ago he played in Scotland. He's in England now. Who is he – and what's the name of the ground at which this picture was taken?

3. Referees are no' whit they were – so moan the fans. Certainly there are few as good as this whistler of the not-so-distant past. With Celtic skipper Billy McNeill is – who?

4. This star gained fame in Scotland – but he wasn't Scottish. His name – and the name of the club in whose colours he was snapped a few years ago?

5. A tough one. Who is the player challenging the two Hearts defenders?

Do you ever think about the grounds you visit? Can you always recognise them? Test your memory with these:

A. What famous ground is this. And what club were the visitors when this picture was taken?

B. At which ground did Celtic's Ken Dalglish score this goal?

C. Where's this – and who are the players?

ANSWERS

REFEREE QUIZ

1 A penalty kick because the offence was committed inside the penalty area.

2. A free kick is awarded because the penalty kicker has played the ball twice before another player has touched it.

3. A corner-kick because you cannot score direct against your own team from a free kick awarded to you.

4. The offender should be sent off because attempting to strike an opponent is just as serious as making contact.

5. Take no action.

6. The referee is within his rights in telling the home club to stop relaying half-time scores as the noise could interfere with the players' and referee's concentration.

7. Yes. In such a position the player is not considered to be interfering with play and if the ball goes into the net a goal must be given. If the ball rebounds from bar or post, though, and the player moves to play it, it must be considered a direct pass with a consequent award of offside.

8. A penalty kick. The referee should have applied the advantage rule – but he didn't and whistled. A penalty must be given because once the whistle has gone the ball is out of play.

9. Yes, it has to be a goal – and pity the referee!

PICTURE QUIZ

1. Peter Cormack, now with Liverpool.

2. Keith McRae, who was transferred from Motherwell to Manchester City. Ground: Fir Park.

3. Hugh Phillips, the famous Lanarkshire referee.

4. Kai Johansen, pictured in his Morton strip before he went to Rangers.

5. Kenny Wilson, of Dumbarton, who left to join Carlisle United and is now with Hamilton Acas.

A. It's Firhill, home of Partick Thistle, and the visitors are Arbroath.

B. Somerset Park, Ayr.

C. It's Cappielow and jousting are Morton's George Anderson and Partick Thistle's Steve Chalmers.

PLAYGROUND TERRORS – and how soccer needs its jesters

Ironically, at a time when football is being criticized for being over-commercialized, too sophisticated and far too serious, I am growing more convinced that the real fan savours the game most because of its schoolboyish attraction.

There is a boy-master relationship about the game which takes the fan away from mundane adult affairs back to the days of his youth when he found it fun to cock a snoot at authority.

Bawling abuse at a referee, for instance, probably makes the supporter imagine he is doing what he dared not do in those happy schoolboy years – threaten his teacher. And certainly most of us look on the referee as a severe dominie out to curb the fun of the players . . . and make the fans unhappy because of harsh decisions which remind them of half-holidays refused or lines given so unjustly.

We also look on managers as the sports masters, the SFA as the officious schools inspectors.

And, seriously, I sometimes believe the authorities act like pompous rectors, taking the fun out of football by banning japes and pranks which we really all relish. I'm all for the playground terrors in soccer, which is becoming far too serious, too concerned with its image.

Take free-kicks, for instance. There is no doubt that the fans love the mischievous, the unusual, cheeky touch. Defenders may moan that they have been conned. But, like schoolboys, we dearly like to see a Smart Alec in action.

Remember that famous donkey-kick by Coventry's Scottish star, little red-haired Willie Carr? He lifted the ball with back-flick of both heels to give a colleague a volleying chance. How that tickled our fancy – if not that of the opponents' defenders. But what happened?

What happened was that outraged masters, in the shape of the FA, outlawed the move. But I was glad last season to see that unabashed Ernie Hunt, who was the colleague to take advantage of Carr's improvisation, is still at it. He came up with a variation to score for his new club, Bristol City, when a team-mate, Don Gillies, formerly of Morton, pushed a boot between Hunt's legs from behind to scoop the ball up for another scoring volley. No doubt this move will also be banned.

I'm sorry, however, that England are giving Scotland a lead in impudent moves. Here, of course, we have Rangers' Tommy McLean, a wizard at taking free-kicks. Often at Kilmarnock he and his colleague, Billy Dickson, scored with outrageous moves from dead-ball situations. I keep thinking Rangers could do more in this line. After all, general manager Willie Waddell was the brains behind the McLean–Dickson moves at Rugby Park and assistant manager, Willie Thornton, when he was

boss of Partick Thistle, dreamed up some controversial free-kick attempts which baffled the opposition and brought delirious joy to the Firhill enthusiasts. Alas, Rangers are perhaps too dignified a club to take part in skulduggery.

But the fans like the unusual. Anyhow, sharp practice is always involved in set-piece free-kicks. Perhaps two or three players are actually needed to be involved with the ball – but the rest will be all out to distract, confuse or even physically impede defenders.

It can be all so simple. Brazil showed that when they scored against England simply by allowing the defensive wall to position itself, then casually placing the ball down a yard to the left of where it should have been, so giving Vavfa a clear shot.

The Brazilians, too, perfected the stratagem of stationing one of their own men on the edge of the wall – and that man ducked away at the last possible second to leave a gap for a shot.

Scotland skipper Billy Bremner was also involved last season in a memorable free-kick.

And how outraged were the faces of the Stoke defenders when the Leeds star scored with all the stealth of a pickpocket. After being tripped, he got up, saw the Stoke keeper had left his line to organize the wall – and calmly pitched the ball into the empty net.

Stoke protested. But the goal stood. And the referee was right. The kick shall be taken, according to the laws, on the referee's signal. Why, after all, should defending teams be allowed breathing space until they are ready? The purpose of a free-kick is to punish the defending team.

Tommy McLean (now with Rangers) and Billy Dickson were terrors to opposing defences when they experimented with new-style free-kicks at Rugby Park, Kilmarnock.

Perhaps the most sensible thing is for the referee to state before the game that if a team want to take a quick free-kick they can, if they accept the risk of losing the ball. Once they ask for the defence to be pushed back 10 yards they must then wait for the referee to resume play. That would give the attack, who are the offended side, the choice of a quick kick at their own risk or a set-piece when everyone is ready.

As I say, I am all for variation. Not only at free-kicks. I remember once watching a Hungarian team take a corner. Eight of the side rushed up to surround the player who was about to take the kick. The opposing side panicked, defenders darting out to leave spaces in front of their own goal. Before they knew what was happening, over came a perfect corner and there to head the ball into the net was the outside-left who had sneaked up out of nowhere, unnoticed. A risk? Sure. But it paid off and gave everyone watching a chance to laugh.

Football needs characters to bring unusual situations.

Yet novelty is going out of the game. It is becoming stereotyped. Not only are characters becoming fewer, so are real stars, stylish individualists who caress the ball, control it magically and rely on craft. Alas, it's the day of the tough guy, the steady defender, the man who doesn't make mistakes, whose main task is to play other more gifted opponents out of the game.

And when I learned that Norman Hunter, of Leeds United, had been chosen by his fellow professionals as their player of the year in England I sighed for football.

Hunter is undoubtedly a good player of his kind. But he is a hard player and if he is

what modern players feel constitutes the star, Heaven help the game – the game which soared to world-wide popularity because of the silken play of great old Scottish inside-forwards, the dribbling wonders of Stanley Matthews, the goal-scoring feats of McGrory, Lawton and Dixie Dean.

But Hunter's choice symbolizes the current thought in football. It must be serious. The aim is stability not success. Try not to lose instead of pinning all your faith in victory. Emphasize defence. Abhor the ball player, the artist, the eccentric genius. And I find it sad that English players admire work-rate, bravery, force, destruction, cold professionalism, rather than flair and skill.

Again, it looks to me like the old school syndrome. The honours go to the steady, serious-minded, hard-working prefect. There are headmasterish frowns for Chirpy Jack, the joker. A decent, honest robust approach is always, in the teacher's mind, better than outstanding talent or brilliance.

In Scotland, too, the honours always seem to go to defenders. In the list of Players of the Year – chosen, I admit, by our Scottish Football Writers Association – there is (up to 1974, that is, when a novel choice was made) only one attacker, Gordon Wallace, of Raith Rovers, in 1968. The others are all defenders – Billy McNeill (Celtic), John Greig (Rangers), Ronnie Simpson (Celtic), Bobby Murdoch (Celtic), Pat Stanton (Hibs), Martin Buchan (Aberdeen), Dave Smith (Rangers) and George Connelly (Celtic).

It is true that there is old-style Scottish skill to be found in most of these players – but I worry and wonder where all the great attackers have gone.

Charlie Cooke in action for Scotland – and how we sigh in Scotland for tricksters of his ability today.

This seems to prove, as in England, the accent is on defence. While we can hail the magnificent attacking play of Celtic, Hibernian and, in a more calculating way, Dundee, we sigh for a new Alex James, a new Hughie Gallacher, a new Tommy Walker, or Gordon Smith or Lawrie Reilly.

I sigh even more deeply for a Peter McKennan, a Bertie Auld, a Charlie Tully, a Tommy McInally, a Charlie Cooke, a Bobby Johnstone – characters who had a schoolboyish, impish sense of humour plus enormous skill – characters who made football such a happy affair . . . and had all other schoolboys, like me and thousands of others, chortling at their antics and making the establishment look silly.

Football, however, is no longer a boys' game. Sometimes I feel it is not even only a game. Certainly it lacks humour and that's why I believe a prize should be awarded to the player who comes up with the trickiest move at a free-kick.

Former Celtic favourite Bertie Auld brought an impish touch to skilful football.

NIGHTMARE IN THE TEXACO CUP: Frank Kopel (Dundee United)

Thirty minutes of poor form in six matches cost Dundee United last season's Texaco Cup.

I believe we would have gone on to win the trophy but for a nightmare half-hour at St James's Park on 19 December 1973.

We had beaten Newcastle United 2–0 in the semi-final first leg at Tannadice a week earlier . . . and we should have won much more convincingly.

We had expected to have to play a waiting game, to struggle for goals. Instead, I headed the opener in 15 minutes from a Tommy Trayner corner and, just six minutes later, Archie Knox added a superb second.

We should have scored more that night at Tannadice in what was surely our best display of the season.

For instance, I still say we should have had a penalty immediately after half-time when Archie Knox was brought down in the box. And there were numerous other occasions when we could have netted.

Still, for 60 minutes of the return game we were sailing through to the final.

We made the worst possible start, losing a goal in just 90 seconds when Keith Robson beat Hamish McAlpine to a through ball and swept it into the net.

Five minutes later, however, we were two ahead on aggregate again when young Andy Gray – what a player this boy will become! – headed in a Tommy Trayner cross.

Then, with 30 minutes left, Newcastle boss Joe Harvey brought on Malcolm Macdonald in a late bid to save the game.

And suddenly, for the first time in six games, we began to struggle. John Tudor headed a second goal in 65 minutes and then, with just 10 minutes left, Supermac forced the tie into extra time with another goal.

I admit we made mistakes in these last 30 minutes, but we were harshly punished.

Even in extra-time we had chances to pull ourselves together and win that place in the final.

But Newcastle keeper Ian McFaul had magnificent saves from Pat Gardner and Archie Knox before the Geordies slammed the door on our challenge with a goal from Tommy Cassidy.

We were doubly sick as we trooped off St James's Park . . . sick because we had come so close and because we had played so well in previous rounds.

The man I felt most sorry for was our boss, Jim McLean, who had done a fantastic job for us in the earlier rounds.

Before the first round he had watched our opponents, Sheffield United, crack five

Frank Kopel, Dundee United. . . . His world collapsed in 30 minutes.

goals past Arsenal in an English League game.

Yet the boss was able to tell us exactly how Sheffield would play against us and how we could beat them. Everything he said was right. We knew every move they would make and we were able to force a 0–0 draw in the first leg at Bramall Lane.

And, when they came to Tannadice for the return, Jim Henry blasted home two great goals as we made United look a very ordinary team.

In the next tie, we got another draw in England, against Leicester City at Filbert Street.

Again the manager had watched our opponents in advance and again his tactics were dead right.

Even when we lost a soft penalty we were never in real trouble and in the second half yours truly scored the equaliser when my shot was deflected past Peter Shilton.

We were again in top form for the second leg, winning with a second-half goal from George Fleming to avenge our defeat by Leicester in the previous season's Texaco Cup.

I'm sorry all the good work had to go for nothing but these six games against English teams did prove a few things for me.

When I played with Manchester United and Blackburn Rovers in the early part of my career I thought English football was tops.

Now, however, I am convinced that Scottish football is just as good. The style is different but our game can be just as effective. I hope Dundee United will have many more chances to prove me right.

Dundee United manager Jim McLean. . . .
He knew the form.

WERE THE OLD-TIMERS BETTER?

The most intriguing argument in football is – and always will be – Were the great old-timers as good as today's heroes? Dads maintain that stars such as Alex James, Alec Jackson, Alan Morton, Billy Steel, George Young and John Thomson were much superior to the men who play today. Sons laugh and declare that yesterday's men could not live with the Billy Bremners, the Kenny Dalglish's, the Denis Laws and the George Connelly's.

This argument, of course, will never be resolved. But last season a man who should know better than most, a man who saw many of the old-time greats and is associated with many of the best of the modern aces, Liverpool and Scotland's Billy Shankly, went into action to say that yesterday's marvellous performers were more talented than the idols of 1974.

Says the down-to-earth Shanks: 'There is nothing new in football. The grounds are the same size. There are 22 players. There is a ball and goal-posts at each end.

'We are told that football is faster now, that the old-time players would never have lived with the speed and pressures of modern soccer.

'But you can't tell me that the men playing now are better footballers than the old stars. And I say that if men like Bob McPhail, Davie Meiklejohn, Jimmy McMenemy and the others were around now they would have been even more exceptional performers than in their heyday.

'With the benefits of the latest training methods, up-to-date practice grounds and the incentives – the colossal sums players earn in these modern times – they would have been absolutely sensational in a 'seventies setting, both as footballers and entertainers.

'What skills they had . . . God knows what they would have done to the moderns.

'Who could ever say that there have been better ball masters than Gallacher and James? They were real craftsmen, real cunning men.

'Players like those "made" time to perform their tricks. They could feint and dummy an opponent silly and, like Stan Matthews, they could have you on the floor by just a waggle of their feet or shoulders.'

I agree with Shankly, even though I may stand accused of showing my age. For I feel the old-timers had more individual magic. They had to perform tricks, control the ball and beat opponents – or they were dubbed bad players.

Today football is more methodical, more of a team effort, but the players of yore had more natural talent.

True, they did not have to face the packed goal areas of this age – if they had had to, they might have packed up the game in disgust, as so many fans do nowadays.

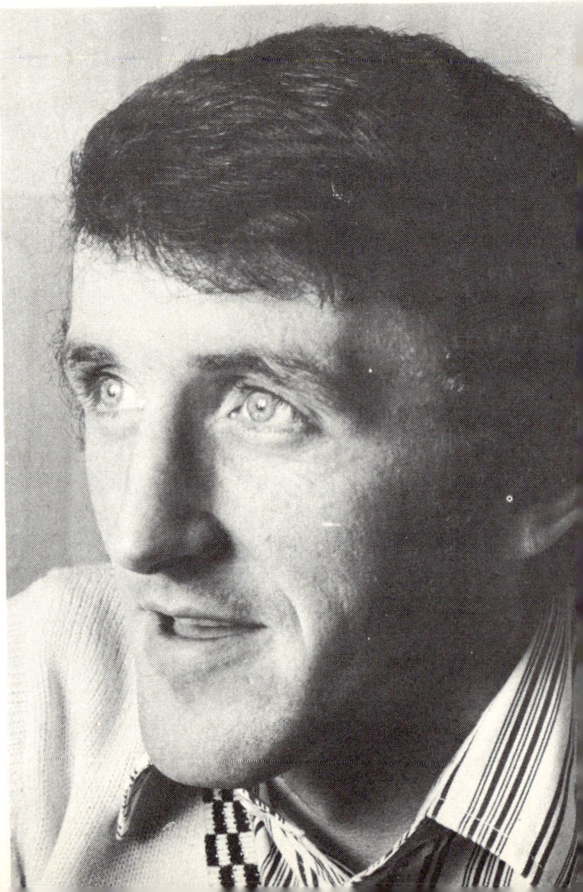

On the other hand, they might have done something about it – for in the old days wingers had the skill to pull out the backs and inside men could pass with accuracy – after, of course, beating an opponent or two. There was none of that crossfield passing and backward running which now allows defenders to funnel back comfortably and pack the goal.

Thank goodness, some of the world's top teams today still play with the verve and intelligence of yesterday. What, for instance, was new-fashioned or complicated about that great Brazilian team which stole all our hearts in Mexico? Defenders had to come off their lines as Jairzinho and Rivelino sped along their wings, with Gerson slinging good long passes in the Andy Cunningham manner, with Tostao and Pele left, as McGrory, Fleming, McFadyen and the great old Scottish leaders were once left, with all the defenders torn away from them.

And Ajax can run in the old-fashioned way.

But in Britain, alas, there is an obsession with team-work, with players and individualism having been stamped on.

Top: The old – and the new. Pictured at Ibrox during Rangers' centenary celebrations are L to R – young Alex O'Hara, a tremendous prospect of today, Willie Woodburn, reckoned the club's greatest centre-half, the incomparable Jim Baxter and old-timer Bob McPhail, one of the best inside-forwards who ever pulled on a light blue shirt.

Far left: Davie Meiklejohn, Rangers skipper who must be included in any football hall of fame.

Left: Danny McGrain . . . one of the most stylish backs of any Celtic era.

How I wish we had some of our old-timers to put the emphasis on skills, not patterns.

What, for instance, would Davie Meiklejohn, that great Ranger, be worth today? He would be the complete middle-man, and not so long ago George Brown, himself a fine wing-half and now a Rangers director, said 'Meek' was the greatest Ranger of all time.

'In attack,' said Mr Brown, 'Davie could spread the most delicate of passes. Yet if he had to fall back in defence he was as hard as nails. And I never knew anyone who could read the game more brilliantly.'

Bob McPhail, who scored 233 Rangers' club goals between 1927 and 1939, was strong as well as skilful – and if he were playing today he would be worth about as much as Denis Law and Joe Jordan put together – for he could score goals as well as make them.

But should we really sigh so much for the old-timers? Believe me, football doesn't change. We are always maintaining the game was better all those years ago. How about this article in a Celtic magazine – written about the Charity Cup Final of May 1918:

'At Hampden we saw the real thing, the genuine article – football that reminded one of the Celtic teams of 20 or 30 years ago, when the game was much younger and ever so much better.

'Football is unlike a good wine in that it does not improve with age. Rather it is like ginger pop, it gets flatter and staler every round of the clock.

'With few exceptions, the players of the present day have neither the physique nor the skill of their predecessors, and while it may seem a trifle ungrateful one has only to compare the present Celtic eleven – the

best in Scotland at that – with others one can recall to realize how little the game has advanced in point of skill.

'To link up mentally past and present Queen's Park, Rangers, Third Lanark, Hibernian and Hearts teams is enough to make one believe that spectacular football is on its last legs.'

Cor!

And yet – playing for Celtic at that time were stars of the magnitude of McMenemy, McNair and Gallagher, whose style would be a revelation to the fans of today.

McMenemy, James called 'Napoleon', was probably the outstanding player of his era. It was said of him that in any game in which he was engaged two footballs should be allowed – one for McMenemy's private use and the other for the common good.

But he was the master of deceptive movement. His facility for shaking off a cloud of opponents by one simple unexpected turn was unequalled. No one excelled him in the art of making an adversary look foolish. He manipulated the ball with the insolent ease of a Harlem Globetrotter and treated the field as a gigantic switchboard, accurately distributing his passes where they were calculated to evoke the best response.

And of Alex McNair it was said that he would have been the perfect subject for a time-and-motion study. No footballer was his peer in the science of achieving the maximum result with the minimum of effort.

The most dashing forward seemed to be mesmerized by his presence. He was gentled along until he had unprofitably crossed the by-line, or alternatively, the ball was withdrawn from him, almost apologetically.

Then, according to the Celtic historian,

Jimmy Johnstone . . . at his best, the wee Celt is a world-class player – and the equal of any of the old-timers.

McNair might elect to do things with it that shot up the blood pressure of the spectators but left him stone cold. His back-passing and dribbling in the goalmouth had the fascination for onlookers that the tight-rope walker in the circus exercises on the audience, who know in their hearts that he is not going to fall but nevertheless await the unexpected. McNair's distribution was uncannily economical, for he was supreme in the art of making the ball do the work.

And that's the secret . . . making the ball do the work.

Perhaps the real reason we revel in the nostalgia of yester-year and weep for stars no longer with us is that dull team-work and organised mathematical defence have stopped genius, have made it useless for gifted players to use the ball as they were once wont.

Perhaps, however, we moan too much. What about Jim Baxter? His career was too short – but his fragrance on the field lives on. Now we are saying he was the greatest, a man to share the throne with James and Morton and Gallagher.

And Billy Steel? Who would deny that in this grim soccer age the wee inside-forward would have been a star of stars?

Lawrie Reilly? His gift for grabbing goals with a half-chance would have made the Hibernian centre-forward, too, a king.

Yet these players have not been retired all that long. In their day, the greybeards said they were not, of course, in the class of Meiklejohn, Stevenson or McGrory.

So it is today.

I must not allow memories to blind me to the fact that there are on football parade even now youngsters who, in the years to come, will be hailed as heroes – Alex O'Hara, Gordon Smith, Jim Pearson and many more.

THE DAY I TOOK A BOW

2 February 1974. That was thc day I was happy to be part of an historic occasion . . . It was the day tiny, part-time Arbroath came to Ibrox and beat the mighty Rangers 3–2, for the first time in their 100-year history.

And my delight had absolutely nothing to do with the fact that I was freed by Rangers a year before that game. I was simply pleased that my decision to become a part-time player at Gayfield after leaving Ibrox had been proved right without any shadow of doubt. It wasn't an easy move for me to make. After all, I had spent 15 years as a full-timer with Dundee and then Rangers.

And for a good part of my spell at Dens Park I had made no secret of my wish to leave the club and join Rangers.

Of course, things don't always work out as well as you hope in football. I am first to admit that my six years at Ibrox were not glorious ones. I never did quite seem to fit into their style of football. Nevertheless, it was a bit of a wrench when I left Rangers, particularly as I had to find a job on the outside of the game and become a part-time footballer for the first time in my career.

But 30 minutes of that match at Ibrox finally convinced me that I had made the right move. I'll never forget the closing 30 minutes of that Rangers–Arbroath match. We were a goal down at half-time, Tommy McLean having put Rangers in front. But we came crashing back into the game with two goals in two minutes, from John Fletcher and Billy Pirie. Rangers equalized with a penalty from Derek Parlane – they had missed one earlier – but then Fletcher scored his second with just three minutes left.

I couldn't resist taking a bow as we came off the field . . . but, as I have already said, there were no sour grapes as far as I was concerned. I was simply happy to be part of a memorable victory. And, let's face it, Rangers were just one of the sides who discovered last season that tiny Arbroath were nobody's push-over.

We did fade slightly towards the end of the season but I don't think any side in the country will treat us with anything other than respect in the future. We are worth a bit of respect, too, having established ourselves as a side always willing to try to play attractive football. The players who really caught the eye last season were experienced men like Eric Sellars and, until his transfer to Aberdeen, Billy Pirie.

They made a brilliant combination up front and it was great to see Eric – a part-timer like the rest of us – up alongside

Andy Penman – he enjoys his part-time football.

players like Dixie Deans, Donald Ford and Jocky Scott in the list of top goal-scorers. He was worth all the goals and the praise because he is a member of a rare breed in modern football – a fast, direct winger who wants to get in there and have a crack at goal.

As I've said, the experienced players took the eye last season but the future of the club looks good, too. I can see several of the young players at Gayfield coming into their own in the near future to ensure that we keep our recently won status in the Scottish game.

As for myself, I hope to be part of the future at Gayfield for some time to come. I certainly enjoy my new life in the game now that I am a part-timer. I probably train as hard as I ever did, even though I only see most of the other lads on match-days.

I intend to go on playing as long as I enjoy the game, as long as I feel I can contribute something to it . . . and I don't think I'll lose that feeling for quite a while. I still get excited every time I walk into the dressing-room on a Saturday no matter who we happen to be playing against.

And, of course, there is still something special about facing the big teams, especially when there is the chance that we might be on our way to another result like that one at Ibrox.

There is nothing like that kind of thing to make a veteran player feel like a first-season youngster again.

THE CRUSADE THAT FAILED...Celtic victims of European Cup hoodlums

It was more like a besieged fort than a luxury hotel. Outside a ring of well-armed, grey-uniformed policemen waited alertly. Tension was written all over the faces of the Celtic players, confined to the Real Monte hotel outside Madrid.

It was no way to prepare for a European Cup semi-final.

But, then, this was no ordinary second leg of a European match.

Celtic manager Jock Stein had never been more angry, more bitter, more anxious to win a game, for he felt that Celtic were going into battle against Atletico Madrid on a soccer crusade – a crusade for honesty, decent football and sportsmanship, a crusade against the hypocrisy, cynicism and thuggery Atletico had brought to the game.

Stein reflected on the brutal play of Atletico in the first leg at Parkhead on 10 April 1974, when three Madrid players had been ordered off and four others cautioned, as he talked about the second leg.

'It was calculated assassination,' he said. 'They didn't come to Parkhead to play football. They came to try to con us out of the game and they got a 0–0 draw.

'Frankly, we should not be here at all. UEFA have sidestepped the issue. They have merely warned Atletico. But they are not really interested in Atletico's savage play in the first leg. They want the second leg to go on at any cost.

'How can we prepare in this atmosphere? Atletico are making out they were the victims in Glasgow and now we are watched wherever we go by police supposed to be protecting us. Our players are jeered at. Threats have been made on my life and on that of Jimmy Johnstone.

'I suppose we have little chance – but how dearly I'd love to win and win by playing football, not descending to the level of Atletico.'

Alas, it was not to be. Celtic were to be beaten in the European Cup semi-final – but not by football. . . .

The whole football world, except that occupied by Spain and the dithering, timid members of UEFA, the Union of European Football Associations, was horrified by the conduct of Atletico at Parkhead in the first leg on 10 April.

It was so unexpected. The Scottish fans still thought about the glorious play and splendid sportsmanship of Real Madrid and they had not been warned that Atletico were different.

They had not realized that the manager of Atletico, the Spanish champions, was Juan Carlos Lorenzo, whose record in football is horrifying.

He was manager of the Argentinian team Sir Alf Ramsey, of England, accused of 'acting like animals'. He was manager of the Italian club, Lazio, whose players he

CAMPARI

incited to attack Arsenal in a dark street after a UEFA Cup-tie. He also hated the British.

The 73,000 crowd at Parkhead were appalled as Atletico, with a hard core of Argentinian players who acted like hooligans, sullied the fair name of football.

Atletico were so nasty, bad-mannered, violent and vicious that Turkish referee Dogan Babacan had to order three of the visitors, Ayala, Diaz and Quique, from the field, and caution another four.

How Celtic maintained discipline against such thuggery must be one of the mysteries of the season. But they had learned the hard way years before against the Argentinian Racing Club in the world club championship in South America that it is fatal to retaliate. Dixie Deans was booked when goalkeeper Reina acted like Olivier when the Celt brushed past him, but otherwise Celtic were admirably behaved.

The Spanish team kicked and tripped and hacked and spat, with their main aim to try to take wee Jimmy Johnstone out of the game.

It was incredible. It was disgraceful. But Atletico got a 0–0 draw, for they packed their defence and just would not allow Celtic to play football.

Even against eight men, Celtic couldn't score but, then, what chance did they have? The Spaniards merely packed their goal and Celtic's lack of punch was obvious.

Trouble flared at the end. Johnstone, despite the abuse he had taken, waited at

Top: Police and Celtic officials try to stop Atletico players assaulting Scottish players at the end of the European Cup semi-final at Parkhead.

Reina, the Atletico goalkeeper . . . cautioned for wasting time at Parkhead.

the entrance to the tunnel to shake hands with opponents. He was brutally assaulted and colleagues and police had to rescue him in the melee that followed.

Atletico went wild. They kicked the Parkhead dressing-room doors and struck an elderly doorman. They, indeed, turned into animals.

But they had succeeded in their objective. They had gained a draw.

It said much for the crowd that they did not take action against the worst hooligans Glasgow has ever seen on a football ground.

The teams for the first leg were:

Celtic: Connaghan, Hay, Brogan, Murray, McNeill, McCluskey, Johnstone, Hood, Deans, Callaghan, Dalglish. Wilson came on for Deans.

Atletico Madrid: Reina, Melo, Ovejero, Benegas, Eusebio, Diaz, Adelardo, Heredia, Irureta, Ayala, Garate.

When television shots of the match were shown, the rest of the soccer world was aghast at the Spanish tactics. Like the Scots, foreign fans demanded that UEFA ban Atletico from the competition.

UEFA funked it. They failed to take any firm and relevant action at a hurriedly convened meeting, at which the members of the disciplinary committee were merely phoned. They warned Atletico and confirmed that six of their players would be banned from the second leg – they had to be, anyhow, because three had been ordered off and the others cautioned twice. They did not even order Atletico to play the second leg on neutral territory.

And Atletico had gone back to Spain, complaining they had been the victims of brutality in Glasgow and started a campaign of hate against Celtic.

Celtic never had a chance in the second leg.

Should they have gone? The directors held a meeting and, bravely, if not wisely, decided they had no alternative but to play in Madrid.

They were subjected to dreadful pressures in a war of nerves. The players were virtually prisoners in their hotel. Jock Stein was warned that he could be the victim of a contrived incident at the stadium Vincente Calderon which would prevent him leaving with his team for home immediately after the game. The Spanish fans were worked into a state of hysteria by evil propaganda.

The scenes at the stadium on 24 April 1974 were horrifying for Celtic. They were booed and jeered and never got a chance to play their real game. Hundreds of armed police were everywhere.

In the end, their lack of finishing let them down as they lost 2–0 and the smooth skills, subtle pacing and crisp shooting of Atletico took them through to the final.

I have never, however, been in such a cauldron of hate. From start to finish the din was indescribable as the 65,000 fans booed Celtic and cheered every move of their heroes.

Yet it was, surprisingly, a splendid and dramatic game, spiced with fine football from both sides. Celtic, despite all the hate, played well in the first half and might have taken the lead.

Atletico, however, paced the game better and scored near the end through Garate and Adelardo. There was a suspicion of offside about both goals – but what would have happened to Swiss referee Paul Scheurer had he disallowed them?

Far left: Celtic skipper Billy McNeill . . . 'I never played in a tougher game.'

Celtic striker Dixie Deans . . . cautioned for brushing past goalkeeper Reina.

As the Celtic players said as they thankfully climbed into their plane for home: 'Perhaps it's just as well we didn't win. We would have all been in the nearby river.'

Celtic: Connaghan, McGrain, Brogan, Hay, McNeill, McCluskey, Johnstone, Murray, Dalglish, Hood, Lennox. *Subs:* Deans, Hunter, Wilson, Callaghan.

Atletico: Reina, Benegas, Heredia, Eusebio, Capon, Adelardo, Luis, Irureta, Ufarte, Garate, Becerra.

Celtic were again out of the European Cup. Perhaps they didn't really deserve to win it. They had struggled in the earlier rounds against Vejle, of Denmark, and Basle, of Switzerland, although they had won easily against Turku of Finland. They lacked finishing power and undoubtedly Atletico were the better team in the second half of the second leg.

But Celtic never had a chance. And the name of Atletico Madrid and manager Lorenzo, for whom a special place should be reserved in football's chamber of horrors, will stink for ever.

There must be a clean-up by UEFA – and in UEFA. If Lorenzo's alarming reputation is so well established by now, what can you say of the clubs – Lazio, San Lorenzo de Almagro of Argentina and Atletico Madrid – who hired him and became accomplices after the fact?

Celtic chairman Desmond White summed it up later when he said: 'When Lorenzo came to Glasgow with his paid assassins he murdered the good name of football. It is to the everlasting credit of Celtic fans that you did not take up the challenge and behaved like true supporters.'

Undoubtedly Atletico had the most cynical and ruthless approach to a game ever known in football.

They will go down in history as the pickpockets of the game. They conned their way into the final – and a disgraceful aspect of their behaviour was that they played brilliant, sophisticated attractive soccer to beat Celtic in Madrid.

To the decent football fan, however, no matter what nationality, they will always be known as the crooks of the game.

How can anyone admire them when the whole world knows that, despite the skill of their team, they had not the guts, the confidence or the character to go to Parkhead to try to match Celtic at football – at which they might well have won?

They had to resort to dishonesty, to trickery. At Parkhead they played only half their first team, loaded it with thugs, tried to foul Celtic out of the tie, did everything in their power to provoke Scottish players and fans – and hoped for a break-in which would see them get the victory.

As English reporter Brian James, who saw the Madrid tie, said; 'This was crime victorious.' And he was right. And UEFA must at once set up orders which will ensure there will never be a repeat.

So relieved were Celtic to leave Spain unscathed, as Brian James said, that we missed the horrifying point: the victims were getting out safely but it was the villains who had won.

There is no doubt in my mind that Lorenzo cynically planned his brutal campaign. It was easy to be amazed and indignant about Atletico's dreadful tactics in Glasgow and to feel a degree of comfort when UEFA banned their six offending players from the return.

But Atletico planned for this. The six banned were not top players. It was a calculated risk. They were the kamikaza pilots. Out to destroy. And if they could take an opposing player off with them so much the better.

Stein was bitter: 'Atletico succeeded in turning the tie into a one-leg match. They didn't allow us to play in the first game, brought on all their stars for the second, played with style and didn't foul – they couldn't afford to – and decided the game by their real team on their own ground in one game.'

Celtic suffered as never before. They could not risk taking any supporters to Spain. They were harassed from start to finish.

Madrid, the city which gave us the great Real Madrid, has now established itself as the birthplace of football's nastiest side.

They are the club who woo you with champagne and spit in your face almost at the same time and they may have set a precedent which will be copied by other ruthless clubs who want to win at all costs.

They will forever be known as the hoodlums of soccer.

A top star for Spain's Atletico was the splendid centre-forward, Garate.

ERIA
TV

THE PLAYERS OF THE YEAR – they gave us the happiest night of the year

History was made by the Scottish Football Writers Association at the end of season 1973–74. They named as their Player of the Year not one star – but a team of stars.

The team who gave the Scottish football fans their happiest night of the year.

The team who beat Czechoslovakia at Hampden on 26 September 1973 and took Scotland to the final stages of the World Cup for the first time since Sweden in 1958.

It was a popular choice, for these players of the year will always be remembered for this epic occasion. . . .

The only pity was that the thousands of fans who helped to make it couldn't have been honoured as well. For they played their part in helping their country on to Germany.

This is the story.

They wouldn't leave, they couldn't leave. They had to stay on and on at Hampden and make our grim old fortress of a stadium a gay, wonderful, colourful arena of noise and waving standards.

Oh, that magnificent Scottish crowd, the greatest in the world, paying tribute to the most courageous Scottish team I have seen.

26 September – a fantastic, emotional night, our greatest soccer night of a decade.

The night Scotland battled through at last to the finals of the World Cup in Munich after a cliff-hanging, palpitating struggle in which hopes soared and plummetted.

But smiling through in the end came Scottish grit, Scottish guts and Scottish skill.

I'll never forget that night, a night which ended with scenes of tremendous jubilation. . . .

With Denis Law lying face down on the turf, having given his all. . . .

With Billy Bremner dashing into the Hampden tunnel to bring on manager Willie Ormond to run a lap of honour in front of the adoring, 100,000 weeping, laughing, shouting fans who had shown no club favour but had bellowed non-stop from start to finish for Scotland.

Under the bright new floodlights, Bremner's Scotland provided an epic.

Scotland had to win because if they failed at home no one gave them any chance of winning the next game in Bratislava.

It started predictably. Scotland all out for the vital goal. The white-shirted Czechs, not one whit dismayed by the frightening Hampden roar, defending stoutly, ruthlessly.

Shouts of rage filled the air as one tough foul followed another. By half-time the crime count was: Czechoslovakia 20 fouls, Scotland 8.

The Scots, however, refused to be intimidated.

Sometimes they shook their heads. For Viktor was heroic in the Czech goal. He made one fantastic save after another. Then

Scotland were refused what every fan believed to be a blatant penalty – when mesmerizing Tommy Hutchison, a weaving wizard, was pulled down in the box. The referee merely waved on play.

Then came tragedy. In 33 minutes the Czechs at last broke out. Neboda flashed in a 35-yard shot from an acute angle on the right.

It was a nightmare for goalkeeper Alistair Hunter. He got a hand to the ball but it slipped past his groping fingers and into the net.

Were the supporters dismayed? Were the players? Not on your life. Awe-inspiring skipper Billy Bremner put new life into his troops. The players redoubled their efforts.

And in 41 minutes burly Jim Holton endeared himself for ever to the Scottish fans by equalizing. The giant centre-half towered over everyone in the Czech penalty area to head a corner into the net.

An unknown eight months before with Shrewsbury before going to Manchester United and getting his Scotland chance, Holton said: 'It was my best moment in football. I had started to come up for dead ball situations because we could see they were struggling a bit in the air. We were sure we could get a goal from the air and that's how it worked out following the corner.'

And so to an even more pulsating second half.

Tired as they were, the Scots continued to press. Manager Ormond took off Kenny Dalglish, who had done so well, and brought on the tall Joe Jordan.

And that brought the Hampden Roar of the century.

Audacious Willie Morgan got the ball on the right, crossed, and with a diving header which will be remembered for all time Jordan hurled himself at the ball to grab the goal that took us to Germany.

Jordan was another unknown with Morton until he became a bright attacker for Leeds. He said of his goal that meant so much: 'I was told to play up alongside Denis Law and to look for the ball in the air. I had one header before the goal came but I mistimed it. Then I went for the ball the next time and got it just right. It was the most fantastic moment of my football life.'

So it all came out right. The dream came true. Scotland had qualified for the World Cup at last – and, on the night of 26 September, that was all that mattered.

No wonder the football writers chose that gallant twelve to be their players of the year, and no wonder I can never forget the crowd, whose support inspired the team.

So let's remember these names with pride . . .

Alistair Hunter, Danny McGrain, Sandy Jardine, Billy Bremner, Jim Holton, George Connelly, Willie Morgan, Davie Hay, Denis Law, Ken Dalglish, Tom Hutchison, Joe Jordan.

THE HAPPIEST PICTURES OF THE YEAR

These are the pictures we'll gaze on time after time. They are the happiest pictures of season 1973–1974 – because they are the pictures which bring to life one of Scotland's real triumphs, victory over Czechoslovakia at Hampden to take us at last to the World Cup finals.

Top left: The goal that did it. Even heroic Czech goalkeeper Viktor can't stop Joe Jordan scoring the victory goal.

Congratulations for Joe Jordan as his colleagues go wild with delight.

Over: Courageous captain Billy Bremner, in Czech shirt, is chaired into the pavilion.

Right: The cameramen get the picture that shows manager Ormond and skipper Bremner in happy pose.

Bottom right: The snap that sums it all up – all the Scotland joy.

Below: Manager Willie Ormond takes his bow after Scotland beat Czechoslovakia.

THE CUP FINAL DRAMA

The players of Dundee United were blazing mad. There they were, high and dry in the final of the Scottish Cup, having played with skill and style all the 1973–74 season – and yet they had been written off long before the big game was due on 4 May at Hampden as rank outsiders.

The Tangerine Terrors, as they were known even in places outside Tayside, felt the bookmakers' odds of 6 to 1 were insulting. They were aggrieved with neutral fans who reckoned manager Jim McLean's team were underdogs. Most of all they were annoyed with fellow professionals who had publicly written them off.

It was true they were meeting hot favourites Celtic – Celtic, who had just won their ninth League championship in a row, Celtic, who were far and away the outstanding team in Scotland, if not all of Britain, Celtic, who had made a monopoly of reaching Scottish Cup Finals.

It was true their blend hardly seemed ideal for a final – key players in their teens, several veterans and a 37-year-old Skipper, Doug Smith.

Manager McLean, the man they call Mr Perfection in Dundee, member of Scotland's most famous footballing family and a talented tactician, was, however, convinced his side were in with a splendid chance.

He said: 'We have faith and confidence. While we have had the luck of the draw in getting as far as the final, we are at Hampden and we will make the most of the chance.

'We have in young Andy Gray one of the greatest strikers in Scottish football and even if he isn't 100 per cent sharp after a cartilage operation he is still a potential matchwinner for he will run and chase all day and he can score vital goals. He displayed that against Hearts in the semi-final with a decisive goal in the replay.'

And McLean promised the fans that it would be a tremendous final, with United playing their own game and going for goals.

Down at Seamill, the bracing village on the Firth of Clyde where Celtic for years have prepared for big matches, there was anxiety.

Manager Jock Stein kept secret the fact that he had half a team suffering from influenza and were unable to train.

While Celtic had just won the League flag by drawing with Falkirk the Saturday before, some of the players were still upset by their traumatic experience in the European Cup semi-final against Atletico Madrid, who had pulled out every evil trick in the soccer book to win, and the champions had lost much of their gloss.

Top: It's that victory spirit. Celtic skipper Billy McNeill shows his elation at winning the Scottish Cup – even though taking a winners' medal is nothing new for the Parkhead hero.

The cup that cheers! Celtic players and officials celebrate their Hampden victory.

Stein acknowledged, too, that Dundee United were a fine team. He said: 'I have listened all week about how much Celtic have accomplished and how little United have won. As far as we are concerned we look on Dundee United as strong opponents and we will treat them as we treat all opponents, by trying to beat them. They may have little to show on the record books but we still respect them and they are capable of generating a very good type of game.

'Anyhow, we want to win this final. We have lost a few League Cups recently as well as the Drybrough, but our record in the Scottish is good and we intend to keep it that way.

'We want to pull off the double of League and Cup. If we do that this will have been one of our most successful seasons.

'We have faced setbacks and injuries and at various times we have been without Brian McLaughlin, who looked so good at the start, Danny McGrain, Bobby Lennox and Davie Hay, and Jimmy Johnstone has only come good towards the end of the season.'

If Celtic were reckoned favourites, United had class – and it looked as though this could be a final of skill and colour.

A crowd of 75,959 turned up at Hampden to see the 1974 Scottish Cup Final and the teams lined up like this:

Celtic: Connaghan, McGrain, Brogan, Murray, McNeill, McCluskey, Johnstone, Hood, Deans, Hay, Dalglish. *Subs:* Lennox, Callaghan.

Dundee United: Davie, Gardner, Kopel, Copland, D. Smith, W. Smith, Payne, Knox, Gray, Fleming, Houston. *Subs:* Traynor, Rolland.

Referee: J. W. Paterson (Bothwell).

Celtic fans were anxious at the start and the way United played gave the men in green and white favours little hope that in a wonderful five minutes their heroes would wrap up the game.

In the first minute, former Dundee and Rangers player, Doug Houston, had an excellent chance but, with no one between him and goalkeeper Denis Connaghan, who had taken over the first-team spot from Alistair Hunter in the Celtic scheme, he sliced a right-foot shot wide.

United were stroking the ball accurately and it took the Celts some time to get into their stride. Once the old guard in green and white pushed back the thrusts of the tangerine, however, the United goal came under heavy fire. From a free kick just outside the penalty area, there was a thrilling familiar sight – that of Celtic skipper Billy McNeill soaring through the air to head a Harry Hood ball just wide.

Then a real touch of class from Kenny Dalglish had the fans applauding. He made an opening for himself with a delicate flick, ran round Pat Gardner, but didn't hit his parting shot hard enough to worry Sandy Davie.

Frank Kopel gave young Andy Gray his first chance to show his skills with a fine pass down the right. The youngster, who was being watched by Tottenham Hotspur, seemed so surprised by his good fortune that he fell, but he recovered well to worry the Celtic defence with a swift thrust.

Just as the game seemed to be developing into a great cup final, Celtic, despite the fact that several players, still feeling the effects of influenza, didn't look 100 per cent fit, produced two killer punches inside five minutes.

It was a depressing situation for United who, as manager McLean had promised, had taken the game to Celtic, spraying the ball about to such effect that Celtic, despite several flashes, could not build up their usual rhythm.

As Walter Smith and George Fleming nursed the ball through the midfield, Celtic began to miskick in defence. Anxious, they by-passed the middle and tried to find their runners with long balls.

It seemed a futile exercise – until the 20th minute, the minute in which United's fate was sealed.

The goal was started by a magnificent piece of work by Dixie Deans. With his back to the goal, he gathered an awkwardly-bouncing ball. He beat two defenders on the turn and sent forward a neat lob. The United defence was flustered. Not Harry Hood. Lurking where the defenders couldn't see him, it seemed, he suddenly moved forward and nodded the bouncing ball over the head of the desperately advancing Davie.

That was all Celtic needed. That gave them back their confidence and poise. United sagged and five minutes later the final was practically over.

This time wee Jimmy Johnstone, who had jinked back to greatness for Celtic, started the move. And Hood the great joined in. Harry took Johnstone's neat pass, cut through cleverly before giving the winger the ball back. Johnstone pushed the ball out to Steve Murray and the former Dundee and Aberdeen player shot quickly past Davie to put Celtic two up.

These two swift blows knocked the Dundee team out of the game and Celtic, with such a comforting and unexpected lead, settled to play fascinating football, so relaxed that it might have been better sited on a practice pitch.

Yet some of their play at this stage was of vintage quality.

United, outclassed for a spell, hit back and, valiantly, Archie Knox went near with a blistering 30-yard shot.

Three minutes from the interval it should have been over but, unaccountably, Dalglish, playing so marvellously, missed an easy chance.

As the interval whistle went, Celtic were playing with a haughty nonchalance and United were reduced to the role of onlookers.

But the scene changed again when the second half began and, to their eternal credit, the gallants from Tayside made a brilliant start.

Theirs was a frightening task. Two goals down. Their first Hampden final. But manager McLean comforted them and inspired them with a half-time pep talk and his brave words had an effect.

Far from looking no-hopers, United began the second period with vicious attacks and twice they came within an ace of scoring.

The Celtic defence floundered in this stirring start. First Gray showed what a fine prospect he is by darting in to head towards goal a cross from point-blank range. But Denis Connaghan made the save of a lifetime – an incredible reflex stop which saved a certain goal. Then the new Denis took time off to tell off his colleagues for allowing Gray to get the chance!

Minutes later, however, even the competent Connaghan was beaten by a savage shot from Knox. Celtic's luck was still in. The ball hit Billy McNeill on the head as he sat on the ground and bounced clear.

United, who have a considerable reputation as a second-half side, were giving the fans their money's-worth.

Yet Celtic cleverly contained that spurt of United adventure and turned the play of their opponents across the field. It grew

monotonous for United had shot their bolt.

Both teams made substitutions – Tom Callaghan replacing McGrain and Andy Rolland coming on for teenager Graeme Payne.

Again it was Celtic in command and Dalglish and Johnstone both missed chances. In a late bid to save the game, United sent on the speedy Tommy Traynor for Doug Smith, but Celtic could not be moved.

Celtic played it professionally. It was not exciting – but it was competent. United could do nothing against the solid defence.

And terracing trouble, with bottles and cans flying and the police and ambulancemen having a hectic time, erupted as the game degenerated into boredom.

United's last gamble failed. Traynor made no difference to the game's pattern. And, with the referee looking at his watch, Dixie Deans scored a third for Celtic after Dalglish made amends for his missed chances by making a splendid opening after an imaginative run.

So it was 3–0 for Celtic and they deserved their win, even if by their own standards their football had been dull. But in those five wonderful minutes in the first half Celtic had scored two fine goals and played football of the highest calibre.

United took great credit, however, and the final was played in a sporting manner.

It was the 23rd time Celtic had won the Scottish Cup, their fourth final victory in six years. Consolation for Dundee United was that they had won a place in the European Cup-winners Cup.

Said Jim McLean sadly: 'There were never three goals in it. We might have turned the game just after half-time but an out of the world save by Denis Connaghan prevented Andy Gray from scoring.'

Controversy broke out after the game. Celtic players ran to both ends of the ground to salute their fans before the official cup presentation – and that didn't please some members of the SFA who have banned teams doing a lap of honour after a Scottish Cup Final. But Jock Stein said: 'We didn't do a lap of honour. The players acknowledged the fans.'

But our cup final sadly needs a touch of glamour – and most people thought Celtic did the right thing.

Perhaps the most disappointed man at Hampden was United's Doug Houston.

Doug had hoped his worst-ever season would end happily – but it was not to be and there was to be no winner's badge for the cultured Houston.

It has been a complicated year for the player. Just a year before he had been transferred from Dundee to Rangers for £30,000 – but the move didn't work out and he moved to United.

But Doug confessed that he had never been on a winning side at Hampden since he left Queen's Park to join Dundee in 1962.

And in 1974 it was his sixth time back on the old ground. Every time he appeared on a major occasion it was against Celtic – and the best he ever managed was a 0–0 draw in a Scottish Cup semi-final.

United, nevertheless, had shown at Hampden that they have class and they certainly did not let their supporters down.

Top: 'Well done, wee man.' Manager Jock Stein has words of praise for Jimmy Johnstone at Hampden.

Dundee United defender Frank Kopel tries to stop Celtic's Kenny Dalglish in a Hampden raid.

WEEP FOR THE WINGERS
by Jimmy Wilson (Dundee)

When my playing career comes to an end there will be no great wingers left in world football.

Don't jump to conclusions when you read this. Don't start calling me a big-headed so-and-so, because I certainly don't mean that I am the last of the great wingers.

What I do mean is that, in 15 years with Newcastle, Morton, Aberdeen, Motherwell and Dundee, I have seen the natural wingers gradually phased out of the game. And it cannot be long before the winger is as extinct as the dinosaur.

It is a sad, sweeping statement but I cannot see it any other way. And the football fan will be the real loser when it happens.

Apart from seeing someone score with a superb header or a 30-yard shot, there is nothing more exciting than a winger beating a couple of men and whipping the ball back from the by-line. I love doing it . . . I love seeing it.

I advise anyone who shares this view to get along to their local ground now because they will be having their last look at a dying art.

The so-called progress in the game over recent years has already killed off some of the really great wingers, the magnificent entertainers.

Look at Rangers. I rated Alex Scott and Willie Henderson two of the finest wingers in Scotland. But the close-marking that developed in the 'sixties cut Henderson off in his prime.

Willie was terrific when he picked the ball up around halfway, got his head down, and headed for that by-line.

That was in the days when the full-back did much more pivoting behind the centre-half. But his days were numbered when another centre-half started pivoting round the centre-half.

This allowed the opposing full-back to mark more closely and gradually the winger was forced to move into his own half and start his operations there. In other words, a winger became a midfield player.

Rangers were not, of course, the only club who faced that problem. And some players manage to adapt to the new role better than others.

Celtic's Jimmy Johnstone has stayed at the top but you could hardly call him a winger any more.

Scotland have probably done more in an effort to preserve good, old-fashioned wing play than most other countries. Sir Alf Ramsey killed it off in England in the mid-'sixties, even the less developed football nations have climbed on the defensive band-wagon.

I know this from my experiences in South

Africa where I had a brief spell with Maritzburg, of Durban.

I left Dundee at the end of season 1972–73 and played half a season in South African football before returning to Dens Park.

The football was of a poorer standard but the tactics were defensive. The only different approach they had to the game was the use of WITCH DOCTORS.

No kidding, they actually used witch doctors to help them before important games. And it didn't just happen with one or two clubs. As far as I know they all used magic at times.

In one of my last games out there, Maritzburg had to win to finish in the top four in the league – and we all had to wash our faces in magic water before the kick-off.

And we won. By 4–0. But before every manager in Scotland goes on a scouting safari to the African jungle, let me tell you I wasn't completely sold on the idea.

Because, in a previous game, we had been told to rub a magic solution on our boots. It didn't work so well . . . we lost.

I returned to Scotland at just the right time, when Dundee were shaping up for victory in the League Cup.

I missed the early rounds but came into the side for the knock-out games. I was upset, naturally, when I was left out of the side that beat Celtic 1–0 in the Final at Hampden but I have been in the game too long to be broken-hearted by things like that.

Right: Jimmy Wilson says wingers are a dying race – but Ayr United's John Doyle still sparkles on the touchline.

Far right: Jimmy Wilson, still sparkling on the Dundee wing after a long and distinguished career. Behind Jimmy is the skilful Jocky Scott.

I didn't have a medal to show for my efforts but that didn't stop me from enjoying the celebration party after the game had been won with that great goal from Gordon Wallace.

And I was delighted that other players who have given a lot to the game in Scotland at last had something to show for their work.

It was easily Dundee's best season in years with players like Thomson Allan, Bobby Robinson, Jocky Scott and John Duncan really making it big.

Jocky and John were the two most improved players at Dens Park. I always knew Jocky had it in him . . . but I must admit John Duncan made me take back a few things.

In past seasons, he was always a player who judged performances on personal achievements. If the team lost 5–1 and he scored the goal he thought he had played well.

But all that changed last season. He began to fight far harder and in my opinion he became just about the most complete centre-forward in Scotland.

Of course, we came so close to finishing the season in another blaze of glory. Our new-found professionalism gave us Scottish Cup victories over Aberdeen, Rangers and Hibs.

Sadly, we didn't hit our true form in the semi-final against Celtic at Hampden in the game that was billed as the Final before the Final.

Top: There's a great winger among the Clyde stars of the not so recent past seen here having a break from football. Can you spot him? He's George Herd, a dazzling performer, second from the left. The others are Cameron, Colrain, McCulloch and Wilson.

A good winger needs a clever inside-forward. Meet a fine partnership which will bring sighs from the Rangers' fans. Winger Willie Henderson was among the world's best and Jorn Sorensen provided fine passes.

JUST A DREAM AWAY
Scotland out of luck in the World Cup

From a tour de farce to tunes of glory – that was the story of Scotland in the 1974 World Cup. An old familiar story. An old sad story. But this time there were at last signs that Scotland had learned lessons, had held her head high in the end. And the brave squad who returned to Glasgow after being unluckily eliminated deserved the heroes' welcome given to them at Abbotsinch airport.

Scotland were unbeaten in the World Cup – but still they went out and that, to me, showed that a new method is needed for the next tournament, a fairer method.

The Scots improved in every game, first beating Zaire and drawing with Brazil and Yugoslavia – two matches in which the players had no luck.

At the end, Scotland were as sturdy a team as any left in the competition.

But there is still much Scotland have to do if they are ever to win the game's premier honour. Manager Willie Ormond did a wonderful job – but in a World Cup he must have more assistance. Compared with other countries, we are frugal and leave far too much to one manager and two trainers.

And certainly we must try to maintain discipline from the start.

It says much for the spirit of Scotland's players that they made a hit after one of the most amazing starts to a World Cup campaign any side ever accomplished.

At one stage the tour – which turned into a tour de farce on trips to Belgium and Norway – reached for me such a peak of hilarity, especially in Oslo, that the combined talents of Jaques Tatti and Charlie Chaplin were by comparison the acme of amateurism.

While ace Scottish players, who had hardly done Scotland's image much good, relaxed in the smiles of SFA authority, the officials ponderously came to a highly important disciplinary decision.

They made up their minds that a journalist had really been a bad boy and banned my colleague, John Mackenzie, of the Scottish *Daily Express*, from flying in their chartered aircraft for the rest of the trip.

They considered an article written by him criticising the conduct of Billy Bremner and Jimmy Johnstone, both reprimanded by the SFA for a breach of discipline, was not good enough and Mackenzie had his fingers rapped.

This banning was the anti-climax to days of soccer astonishment. On a trip which was supposed to be a warm-up rehearsal for the World Cup, the Scottish players, having bemoaned the efforts of agent Bob Bain to get them perks to suit their pockets and having shown their displeasure with the SFA by refusing to wear the Roary Scot tie because it was a commercial enterprise of the bosses and not theirs, cheered up on the flight to Belgium on the way to the first tour game.

Joe Jordan heads in Scotland's second goal in the match against Zaire at Dortmund.

Things went well enough, although the hotel in which the party was billeted outside Ghent was situated in a maze of motorways. No one was too worried by the narrow defeat by Belgium for, after all, the exercise was to evolve a pattern to take us to everlasting fame in the World Cup.

An early rise and bus run to Brussels on the Sunday had compensation when the chartered British Airways Trident took off for Norway.

I raise my hat to the crew. This was a champagne flight which would have impressed even Onassis. Most of us took a glass or two. I don't know whether the players did. But when the whole party marched into Oslo airport few were not carrying a bottle of the best wine or half a dozen miniatures or so of liqueurs.

Perhaps it was jet lag or the euphoria of the flight – but no one thought it might be better to collect the nearly tied packages from the players and retain them for celebration after the World Cup had been won.

So skipper Bremner and winger Johnstone obviously sampled the gifts and, possibly displeased by the austere accommodation of their rooms, decided to explore

This sequence of pictures illustrates Bremner's unfortunate miss in the match against Brazil. (*Top left*) With Leao helpless and an open goal in front of him Billy Bremner squeezes in a right-footed shot which (*bottom left*) scrapes past the post. (*Above*) Bremner and Hay are horrified, and the game ended in a goalless draw.

the huge hostel which in winter houses Norwegian students.

Their hardly brisk footsteps took them, surprisingly, to the bar in which dozens of tourists were celebrating a summer holiday week-end.

Bremner had a rather acrimonious argument with one or two Pressmen about what he thought they had written and wee Jimmy, more mellow than the abrasive skipper, felt a chorus of 'Scotland, Scotland' would brighten a smoky atmosphere.

Nothing outrageous, you understand. Simply high spirits.

Manager Willie Ormond, however, wasn't happy when he was told two of his players weren't in their rooms.

He was summoned after other players had tried to tell the happy two that sleep beckoned, rushed into the bar and said simply: 'God, not you two.'

The rest of the scene you may well imagine. Eventually, the two were taken back to their rooms. The morning after brought gloom, profuse apologies to the SFA selection committee who had gravely considered all the facts of the case – and a reprieve because Willie Ormond, a nice wee

Members of the Scottish squad in training at their Weilnau headquarters before the match against Yugoslavia. (*L. to R.*) Bremner, McGrain and Dalglish.

man, had again put his head on the chopping block and appealed to the committee, most of whom had decided enough was enough, and wanted to send the culprits home for this serious breach of discipline, to allow keymen to remain with the party.

As always, the vigilant reporters were quickly aware of yet another escapade which had made Scottish tours top of the bill when fantastic tales of curious incidents abroad are told around the dinner table.

We laughed – but did nothing. Nothing could be reported. Nobody wanted to report it – because, though some don't think so, the Scottish Press are just as eager as anyone to see the World Cup being borne in triumph down Sauchiehall Street.

On Monday, however, serious-faced secretary Willie Allan summoned the Press party and gravely read out the famous statement that two of the players had been reprimanded for a serious breach of discipline.

So action had to be taken. The story had to be told – because the SFA, who had taken no action really against the two players, had made it public.

Would the SFA name the players? Not on your nelly, they said. What, we asked, about the other players, who might be tagged with behaviour? Sorry, murmured the SFA, but that's the statement, take it or leave it.

Well, editors wouldn't leave it. The players were named. Or all the reporters would have been ordered home.

In the midst of all the furore, there was thought of football with practice games being played, Jim Holton recovering from injury and John Blackley being put on the casualty list after a tough tackle.

SFA President Rankin Grimshaw came to the rescue with strong words about everyone pulling together and real stern action being taken against any future offenders of the new learn-to-behave code.

We all applauded the new policy – and then the officials and players read the London editions of the papers which had just been flown in.

They were horrified. Although what they expected the papers to say about the Bremner-Johnstone escapade after they themselves had revealed a breach of discipline, I don't know.

The first the reporters, however, knew about being on the black list came at the practise match on the Tuesday evening.

As we tried to enter the Ulleval stadium to see the team take part in a practice match, we were curtly told: 'The Scottish manager has told us not to let the Scottish Press inside.'

After trying to see what was happening by peering through the barbed wire barriers and noting mainly the cameras of the English BBC team who were allowed in, not being naughty boys and also having paid a sum into the players' perks pool, there was a dramatic confrontation with manager Ormond after the session ended.

Ruddy cheeked Willie paled somewhat when he saw the angry army of Scottish Pressmen. But bravely he told us: 'I did not want to let you in to watch us practise because mainly of what one of you said about the bar incident.

'I am not going to argue with you in front of these Norwegians but I have plenty to say to you and I'll see you all at ten tomorrow.'

If any of us appeared before the beak in fear and trembling that morning, anxiety was soon allayed. Wee Willie can never be furious for long. He was anxious to please, to get on with his task of winning the World Cup – a task plagued with antics which couldn't fail at a burlesque show.

Although he still said he was offended by the tone of the Press articles he had seen, he had also banned the Press from the practice match because he wanted to try out new moves.

'But why,' we asked, 'should you allow Norwegian manager George Curtis to watch you and ban us?'

'Oh, dear,' said Willie, 'I didn't know he was there. He would have been out too if I'd known.'

But he grinned that endearing grin and assured us: 'In future I'll let you know if you can see the training. In 90 per cent of it, you'll be allowed in. Only if we want to try something new will I ask you to leave us alone.'

With happiness practically restored, with rapport established again between officials and villainous Press, Scotland narrowly beat Norway – and we were all set for the World Cup, for which we had qualified gloriously for the first time since 1958.

The players gasped at the tight security measures taken by the German police when they flew into Frankfurt. As the chartered Trident jet whined to a stop on the runway, efficient armed police and troops surrounded the jet. A yellow and blue bus roared out to the plane doors and the Scottish players were given the top VIP security treatment. With a motor cycle escort, the bus, on which was emblazoned the flag of St Andrew, immediately took off for the Rodweil, the Taunus resort at which the Scots were quartered.

Then the squad settled thankfully into the peace of the wooded hills, just like the Trossachs, and manager Ormond got down to the real World Cup campaign.

There were injury worries but, on the other hand, the spirit was right and we all hoped Scotland would rise to the big occasion. They did. No more japes. No more indisciplined outbursts. No side worked harder, in the World Cup of 1974, than Scotland. No side were more dedicated. No side gave the fans a bigger treat. In the hills the Scots felt right at home. It was a picturesque region of mountain, forest and river. The air was like champagne, the people friendly, making a terrific fuss of the Scots.

The first match against the unknowns of Zaire was vital and Scotland received a boost in Frankfurt, for our wonderful tartan-tammied fans gave the squad new pride and determination when they reached the city. Players' nerves were strained, pulses were pounding as the hours crept away to a game we all knew just had to be won. But there they were, as they always are, the lads in the tammies and the kilt, gaily kitted-out, tired from arduous journeys from home – but giving the Scots a tremendous cheer.

Well, we beat Zaire – by 2–0, with goals from Peter Lorimer, a blockbuster, and Joe Jordan. At the time we thought it was a splendid result. Alas, it wasn't. The players froze, thought two goals were enough, and instead of hitting hard at their opponents in the closing stages, decided to tie up the game. That was fatal, as it proved. Another goal against Zaire and we would have qualified for the second round. But Yugoslavia scored nine against Zaire and Brazil, the big disappointment of the early stages, scored three – an odd last goal, with the Zaire keeper injured and making a dreadful hash of a shot. But it was enough to put Scotland out, undefeated – but just one goal short.

Nevertheless, against Brazil and Yugoslavia Scotland played with great skill and great heart. And who could have asked for more? Well, maybe goals.

Anyhow, the noise which reverberated all over World Cup Germany when the end for us came was not that of an avalanche of tartan tears shed by the thousands left for the bravest Scotland team in history. The noise was from the sighs of relief going up from every other country left in the tournament.

Our tragedy was that the team did not receive one break. But the future was brighter on the international scene than it had ever been. We were all proud of the Scots, who had started on a farcical note

A kilted cheer-leader leads a contingent of Scottish supporters.

"EASY"

Bank-Bethmann Bank

Left: Sandy Jardine, rated one of Scotland's best players during the tournament, fails to prevent Karasi scoring Yugoslavia's goal.

Above: Joe Jordan scores the equalizer in the crucial game against Yugoslavia.

but steeled themselves into a team as determined and brave and skilled as any.

The truth is that Scotland might well have gone to the final – though, to be honest, I don't think we had just enough skill, sophistication or enough class players to have won the World Cup – if it hadn't been for that 15 minutes of frozen horror against Zaire.

Against Brazil and Yugoslavia, however, Scotland were positive, courageous, able, sporting, and taking nasty fouls without thought of retaliation – a great step forward for teams who have had too many bristling bantams.

Billy Bremner was our inspiration and, if we had reached the last stages, he might well have been given the award as the best player in the tournament – for he was brilliant.

If we can keep this side together, we can not only become a tremendous power again in football – but we can turn a cycle and have other sides copying our exhilarating, powerful attacking system.

Scotland entertained in the World Cup, went out to win every game. Others didn't. Now we have players of the first class – Bremner, Jardine, Hay, Holton, Harvey. And our fans are magnificent, the best in the world.

With more help for Ormond, a world-wide expert who can analyse the politics of the tournament and a repetition of the 1974 spirit, Scotland can yet reach the top.

These were the Scotland teams in the World Cup of 1974: At Dortmund, on June 14, against Zaire, when Lorimer and Jordan scored in the 2–0 victory: Harvey, Jardine, McGrain, Bremner, Holton, Blackley, Dalglish, Hay, Lorimer, Jordan, Law.

Zaire: Kazadi, Mwepu, Mukombo, Buhamga, Lobilo, Kilasu, Mayanga, Mana, Ndaye, Kidumu, Kakoko. *Referee:* G. Schulenburg, Germany.

At Frankfurt, on 18 June, in the 0–0 draw – Harvey, Jardine, McGrain, Holton, Buchan, Bremner, Hay, Dalglish, Morgan, Jordan, Lorimer.

Brazil: Leao, Nelinho, Pereira, F. Marinho, B. Marinho, Piazza, Rivelino, Cesar, Jairzhinho, Mirandinha, Leivinha. *Referee:* van Gemert, Holland.

At Frankfurt, on 22 June, when Karasi and Jordan scored in the 1–1 draw: Harvey, Jardine, McGrain, Bremner, Holton, Buchan, Morgan, Dalglish, Jordan, Hay, Lorimer.

Yugoslavia: Maric, Buljan, Hadziabdic, Oblak, Katalinski, Bogicevic, Petkovic, Acikomic, Bajevic, Surjak, Dzajic. Karasi was a substitute. *Referee:* J. Archundia, Mexico.